THE RISE STALL

OF TEACHER EDUCATION REFORM

AACTE

MICHAEL FULLAN · GARY GALLUZZO
UNIVERSITY OF TORONTO · GEORGE MASON UNIVERSITY

PATRICIA MORRIS · NANCY WATSON
MORGAN STATE UNIVERSITY · UNIVERSITY OF TORONTO

The American Association of Colleges for Teacher Education is a national, voluntary association of colleges and universities with undergraduate or graduate programs to prepare professional educators. The Association supports programs in data gathering, equity, leadership development, networking, policy analysis, professional issues, and scholarship.

This study was prepared with the help of a Ford Foundation grant in 1995.

The opinions, conclusions, and recommendations expressed in this monograph do not necessarily reflect the views or opinions of the American Association of Colleges for Teacher Education. The AACTE does not endorse or warrant this information. The AACTE is publishing this document to stimulate discussion, study, and experimentation among educators. The reader must evaluate this information in light of the unique circumstances of any particular situation and must determine independently the applicability of this information thereto.

Copies of *The Rise and Stall of Teacher Education Reform* may be ordered from:

AACTE Publications
One Dupont Circle, Suite 610
Washington, DC 20036-1186
WWW: http://www.aacte.org

Single copy for AACTE members: $20   For nonmembers: $25
Please add $5 for shipping and handling

Printed in the United States of America

International Standard Book Number: 0-89333-159-7

CONTENTS

FOREWORD
A BEGINNING OR AN END?

The Holmes Group, with which the substance of this stimulating report by Michael Fullan and his colleagues is concerned, lived in the public eye for 10 years. Its first annual meeting was held in the nation's capital in January 1987, in a blaze of publicity and to the noise of the trumpets of pedagogical war. Ten years later, its last national meeting unrolled (symbolically perhaps) at the crossroads of the nation in the city of St. Louis amidst exhortations to look towards new frontiers and the rich diversity of the United States. At some ontologically obscure moment in Missouri, the Holmes Group was honored with the appropriate obsequies, and its spirit reborn (or perhaps not) in the new form of the Holmes Partnership. These pages tell the story of that evolution, and assess the impact of 10 years of sustained hard work. They give a subtly balanced account of achievement and of failure. Although written as an evaluation for the Ford Foundation, which invested imaginatively in the work of a hardy band of pioneers, this report will be of great interest to a wider public. And not least to those who stubbornly believe that teachers and their quality are the critical element in any sustained educational reform, while wondering anxiously whether much has yet been or even can be achieved in furnishing for the states (and indeed the world) such teachers in the numbers and of the character so urgently needed.

The timing of the publication of the *Rise and Stall* report is propitious, coinciding as it does with a number of initiatives which are in two senses promising—full of promises, as well as of promise. The most central of these welcome initiatives, The National Commission on Teaching and America's Future, is characteristically audacious (its own word) in establishing an overarching goal for the next 10 years: ". . . by the year 2006, America will provide all students in the country with what should be their educational birthright: access to competent, caring, and qualified teachers." The *Rise and Stall* report leaves judiciously suspended in space an answer to the one question that matters: If Holmes did not achieve this noble ambition in the past 10 years (demonstrably much more difficult of an achievement than placing a man on the moon), how much more success will reward its current successors? I assume that the only reason for asking a foreigner to write this brief introductory section must be that I was the only total outsider present at the entrances and exits of the two nodal meetings in Washington and St. Louis, while persevering as an obsessive watcher of Holmes across the intervening decade.

The Holmes Group, as first conceived by Judith Lanier of Michigan State University and a handful of like-minded fellow deans, was an alliance of 100 major research universities in the United States, dedicated to applying the intellectual and material resources of those powerful yet often rigid places to the deep and permanent improvement of the education of teachers. Holmes was to achieve for the education of teachers what Abraham Flexner had accomplished for doctors, albeit without falling into the sinister traps of elitism or, this time around, sacrificing to "professional" ambitions the interests of women and minorities. In the best places, the education of teachers would at last become better (intellectually serious and professionally relevant), while in bad places it would cease. Although the tensions were from the beginning as sharp as they were unavoidable, the key goals were articulated in the most influential of the three Holmes publications, *Tomorrow's Teachers* (1986), and are well summarized in the *Rise and Stall* report.

What is more, in the dawn of 1987, I presumed to tease both the company assembled in Washington and myself by naively asking: "How will observers in exactly 10 years time know whether *it* has happened?" and then proposing six deceptively simple and specific questions to serve as tests for the matching of achievement with ambition. *"It"* was what could be read as the program adumbrated in *Tomorrow's Teachers* "together with the implications which might be legitimately drawn from it. 1997 has now happened, and the last few words of this introduction must of course therefore disinter those dusty 1987 questions, and invite from each reader her or his own responses to them.

Just as a good wine needs no bush, the Fullan et al. report strictly speaking needs no introduction. Indeed, what remains by way of prologue might be more usefully read after rather than before the *Rise and Stall* report which follows. Since the *Rise and Stall* report offers its own nuanced answers to the problematical question of how much Holmes achieved, those answers deserve to be read before my own compressed reactions. *Rise and Stall's* conclusions will be endorsed by most of those who are familiar with the history, now fortified by the assurance that those conclusions are based not on general impressions but on well-defined and -described empirical data. For my own part, the only differences to be proposed would be of proportion and emphasis, flavored perhaps by a more poignant sense of regret that some opportunities—especially in the most recent years—were somehow lost. The most salient change since 1986 has without doubt been the installation of teacher education reform at or near the head of every agenda for educational regeneration: a hitherto neglected or subordinate theme has become dominant. Just as it has emerged as a commonplace that reform cannot be achieved without good teachers, so it has become axiomatic that good teachers need and deserve a first-class preparation. After some real or alleged initial reticence, the pursuit and achievement of greater equity—and the concomitant development of a teaching force more reflective of the accelerating diversity of American society as a whole—has been inserted at the core of teacher education reform. Specifically, the institution and funding of a network of Holmes Scholars, nurturing able members of historic minorities for careers in educational scholarship, has been an impressive and severely practical demonstration of that commitment.

The agenda of the research community has mirrored a cumulative change of emphasis, exemplified by the establishment and growth of a specialist division within the American Educational Research Association and (possibly even more importantly) by the dramatic expansion of participation in research and university-related activities by a host of K–12 teachers. The dismal gulf between the best practicing teachers and the ethereal world of the university has been narrowed, as the rhetorical example of the history of medical education suggested that it must be. The Professional Development School (PDS), the very name of which enjoyed but a shadowy existence in 1987 and which was proposed by Holmes as the metaphorical analog of the teaching hospital, has now become a commonplace of the discourse of reform: so much so that there is a lurking danger of "PDS" becoming a vacuous mantra rather than a carefully specified engine of reform. The late Ed Meade of the Ford Foundation was surely wise (as he so often was) to insist that the Holmes Group should have asserted ownership of the PDS as a complex yet practicable idea, as both the symbol and the engine of a new partnership between theory and practice, and that the Holmes Group should for that very reason have more vigorously resisted the indiscriminate application of the term to just any form of vaguely defined and often aspirational partnership.

The *Rise and Stall* report which follows frankly acknowledges the difficulties of establishing any precise measure of the scale of real change or of attributing to the Holmes Group direct (and still less exclusive) responsibility for such change. However wide and balanced the samples examined, much of the research which validates the conclusions of this report is essentially an inquiry into opinion: into what leaders, advocates, actors, and critics believed happened, or what they wished had happened, or what they felt about the efforts of others. While this collective subjectivity is a common, and perhaps unavoidable, weakness in much educational research and evaluation, there is no reason to resist the conclusions of the *Rise and Stall* report that change was indeed both substantial and widely dispersed throughout university campuses.

Nor is too much time wasted in these pages on disentangling the contribution made directly by Holmes from the persisting efforts of other groups. Across the years under review, the principles and efforts of Holmes, of John Goodlad's network, of the Renaissance Group and of Ted Sizer and his associates (to name but a few) interlocked and reinforced one another. Reform groups are not mutually exclusive sects (even if overzealous advocates sometimes speak as though they were) and in practice most of those propelling university-based teacher reform were content to be eclectic, drawing upon serviceable ideas and supportive networks as their needs dictated. The Holmes Group was a powerful stimulus to reform although it was, of course, content to take as well as to give.

HAS THE WORD

"PROFESSIONAL"

BECOME REDUNDANT?

What, then, of those six questions left hanging in the chilly Washington air in January 1987? Did *"it"* indeed happen? The cryptic questions projected forward to 1997 were:

1. Has the word "professional" become redundant?
2. Are teachers more cheerful?
3. Are principals teachers?
4. Is teacher education perceived as a graduate activity?
5. Has the number of sites been reduced?
6. Have colleges of education changed?

There was, of course, no suggestion that these were the only or even the most important questions; but it was hoped that a future effort to revisit them would give some indication of what had, and what had not, been achieved in the intervening decade.

Has the word "professional" become redundant? The central argument here was that, certainly in the field of education, the word professional had been perilously overused, and especially by unions and other advocates. Of course, it was devoutly to be hoped that teaching would be at least as well-respected as in (some) other countries, that it might acquire a greater control over its own standards, that its practitioners might be better rewarded. But it would be dangerous to turn a slogan into a policy, or (given the current debates on these themes) to imply that teachers wished arrogantly to extract from society the same privileges as doctors or lawyers already enjoyed. Professionalism, not to say professionism, no longer represented self-justifying virtues. Nor was it self-evident that it was dogmatically necessary to assert that teaching was ideally (like medicine) a lifelong career, that the only worthy teachers were those who dedicated their whole working lives to the classroom, or that the only way to prepare teachers was to take them raw at the age of 18 or so, inject them with a preparatory course, and launch them for life. Finally, it was obfuscating to suggest that establishing teaching as a profession presupposed that all teachers were essentially somehow identical, or equally professional. Holmes, like the 1986 Carnegie Forum, argued instead for a more open, varied, flexible, and lifelong pattern of teacher development, and indeed of diversity of role. The blanket term "profession" did not serve these purposes well. Has the word professional become redundant? No.

Are teachers more cheerful? The greater variety and expertise (professionalism if you must) of teachers would allow them more space for creativity, commitment, and autonomy. They would become less Taylorized, less subject to oversight by school boards or regulation by an anxious state, more confident in their knowledge and skills. Are they? No.

Are principals teachers? Any foreign observer of American schools in the 1980s would have been struck by the schism between principals and teachers. Principals were not, in spirit and by formal qualification, the best of the teachers: rather, they were seeking to join a quite different corporation, that of the administrators. If they wished to advance far in that supposedly superior cadre, then they would need higher degrees in administration, which colleges of education were likely too happy to provide. Principalship and its subordinate branches was the conventional means of escape from the classroom. The Holmes view of educational leadership was by contrast one in which teaching and learning were more important than the banausic tasks of accountancy and management. This was an integral part of a coherent policy, further articulated in later publications, affirming the integrity of the educating professions, within which there would be a healthy continuity of instructors (not, it must be said, a happy term), professional teachers, career professional teachers, counselors, administrators, curriculum developers, researchers. Curiously, this simple idea never took root. In spite of the strenuous efforts of a handful of zealots, the Holmes Group never succeeded (least of all in the discussions leading up to its final publication) in shifting from a monocular preoccupation with "teachers" (in the antique sense) to a broader emphasis upon educating all those who are concerned with the learning of young people. Are principals teachers? Evidently not.

Is teacher education perceived as a graduate activity? The Holmes Group originally argued that it must be, then lost its nerve. The economic and logistic, rather than the intellectual, argument prevailed and the status quo was too deeply entrenched. It at first believed that teacher education should be disentangled from the work of the arts and sciences, whose proper business would then be the provision of a sound general education appropriate for all citizens, of course including future teachers. This greater clarity of function would eliminate much of the territorial friction between education and the arts and sciences, sharpen the focus of graduate programs of professional education, clarify a distinction between the teaching of (say) mathematics and the teaching of the teaching of math. The Holmes Group was not originally conceived (and this is one of the few points on which I would wish to adjust the argument of the report) as a pressure group of colleges of education, and still less of their deans. The original invitations were addressed to principal academic officers of major universities, and not only to education deans. The regressive drift from a commitment to making teacher education a graduate activity muddied the waters. The authors of the report, correctly in view of the intervening history, sought few respondents outside the colleges of education and the public school teachers associated with them. The first time I heard the provost of a major university address members of the group was at its first meeting: that was also the last time. Answer to this question: No, or not often.

Has the number of sites been reduced? The Holmes Group honestly believed that in 1986 there was too much teacher education. It was a paradox of the American scene in the 1970s that as the demand for new teachers declined the number of universities and colleges offering teacher education increased. Making teacher education more intellectually serious, linking it properly through the PDS to the world of practice, required the elimination of substandard programs. This lordly insistence, sometimes (to be fair) proceeding from high universities which had long since ceased to take the activity seriously, was not universally applauded. But, for once, the Flexner precedent was appropriate, or so Holmes believed. Teacher education, for reasons of prestige as well as of quality, needed to be more concentrated in major research universities. But, of course, the word elitism (unlike leadership or quality) has a most unpleasant smell. The line could not be held without causing division and dissension: especially when principles of equity were so obviously and necessarily involved. Has the number of sites been reduced? No.

Finally, have colleges of education changed? It is around this question that some of the most illuminating pages of the report revolve. Of course, the colleges would incontrovertibly have changed had it been possible (or ultimately thought desirable) for teacher education itself to become, at least in most of the major universities, a graduate activity. They would have changed if the educating of career professional teachers (under whatever name) had challenged the supremacy of other more traditional forms of graduate education. They would have changed, and of course may still so do, if the PDS and parallel innovations lead to the generation of new styles of scholarship as well as of rigorous preparation for *all* the educating professions. The report itself stresses the importance, as well as the ferocious difficulty, of "reculturing" the colleges. Such an enterprise requires the systematic dislocation of a whole array of vested interests. Within the academy, education (like law, medicine, business, yet in a way appropriate to itself) still needs to develop and apply new criteria for tenure, promotion, the allocation of workloads and of prestige. The authors of the report point discreetly towards some of the reasons for a loss of momentum within the Holmes Group, and especially in the processes leading to the publication of its third and least impressive document. It was easier (if still difficult) to argue persuasively and to act on the reform of teaching and of schools, and the first two Holmes books did just that. The effort stalled (which is not to say terminated) when the colleges and schools of education had to think seriously about reforming themselves. They will change only when they really wish to, and not enough yet do.

HARRY JUDGE
OXFORD, ENGLAND

PREFACE

One of us wrote about teacher education as "society's missed opportunity," and said it had the honor of being simultaneously the worst problem and the best solution in education (Fullan, 1993). Intuitively, if not politically attractive as a *sine qua non* of reforming the public school system, teacher education remains "stalled."

This report characterizes the decade 1985–1995 as a series of false starts in reform of teacher education—promises that could not be maintained. Efforts that began with enthusiasm in the first half of that decade, faltered with discouragement and confusion in the early 1990s.

As it has turned out, the lull has been brief. Out of the still smoldering ashes, teacher education reform has become reignited with a convergence of powerful forces claiming a deeper, allied, comprehensive agenda. As we write, plans are underway to revitalize the Holmes Group renamed as the Holmes Partnership; the National Commission on Teaching and America's Future (1996) has not only produced an excellent report, but has launched comprehensive implementation strategies in 12 states (with others showing interest to join); and major federally sponsored national, multilevel initiatives have been formulated including "A National Partnership for Excellence and Accountability in Teaching" and the reauthorization of Title V of the Higher Education Act, based on a vision to reshape "the profession that shapes America's future."

The main purpose of our report is to raise the question of whether this next decade of reform—1996 into the millennium—will be any different. We say, "Don't be seduced by the political excitement of the day." Reform in teacher education is going to require years of intensive, smart, and hard work at all levels of the system. One could not underestimate the complexity of the challenge.

Teacher education, then, is an incredible, and up to this point, intractable problem. It has proven to be an elusive and slippery agenda. We hope that our contribution will stimulate leaders at all levels to take the current new initiatives all the more seriously, not only for their promise, but also for what will be required to make them stick.

This study, commissioned by the Ford Foundation at the request of the Holmes Group leadership, was originally intended to assess retrospectively the work of the Holmes Group—a national consortium of nearly 100 research universities across the United States. Arguing that teacher education should be more central to the universities' mission, the Holmes Group focused on increasing the quality of programs by connecting them more closely to research on teaching and learning in partnership with schools.

Ford was interested in having an external group examine the impact of its investment in Holmes, as the foundation reflected on the past decade. The bigger purpose, however, was to look ahead. Where was and should the larger field of teacher education be heading in the future? Should the foundation, along with others, reactivate its interests and role in teacher education reform?

In sponsoring this AACTE publication, the Ford Foundation wishes to reach a wider audience. The Holmes Group was emblematic of some of the best efforts over the last decade, but was still not nearly enough. The question now is what will it take to make serious and substantial progress?

Our study focuses on the United States as that was our brief, although many of the basic problems are similar across the world. In Chapter 1, we first present the problem. Briefly, the need to do something about teacher education is reaching crisis proportions. So much of the rest of the education reform agenda depends on a quality teaching force operating under professional working conditions. In Chapter 2, we use the Holmes Group as a case illustration of some of the possibilities and difficulties of accomplishing significant improvements. If one of the better efforts, and Holmes is certainly that, has a hard time making progress, what does that say about the size of the problem? The Holmes case analysis enables us both to understand, in its own right this significant initiative, and to identify the key issues that need to be addressed. Finally, Chapter 3 looks ahead by taking stock of the recent convergence of high-profile plans of action; it allows us to ask again more forcefully: Will this be another cycle of rise and stall, or do we know enough and care enough to really make the core improvements that are required?

The "rise and stall" of momentum is an apt metaphor. Aircraft stall when they run out of lift in attempting to climb at a rate that cannot be supported by the power supplied. Stalling, of course, if unattended to, can result in a fatal crash. But it also presents an opportunity for decisive action to re-energize the power supply—to do things that will generate new sources of energy.

We hope our study will contribute to the debate and to the commitments necessary to, once and for all, bring the teaching profession into its proper, and indeed crucial, place in society. The profession should be a force for quantum and continuous improvements in the performance of the educational system as an agent in societal development. It does not enjoy that role at the present time.

ACKNOWLEDGMENTS

Our thanks to Judith Lanier, who initiated the idea of the study, and to the Ford Foundation (especially Joseph Aguerrebere and Alison Bernstein) for sponsoring the project and for encouraging us to think more broadly. We had tremendous cooperation from the Holmes Group leaders and members, and in particular, we wish to thank Judith Lanier, Frank Murray, and Nancy Zimpher.

We distributed the original draft report of the Holmes assessment to a select number of "readers." While confirming the essence of the findings, these reviewers gave us valuable ideas and insights. Our thanks to Michael Connelly, Linda Darling-Hammond, John Goodlad, Andy Hargreaves, Ken Howey, and

Harry Judge. Our thanks also to Claudia Cuttress who provided great administrative support throughout this study culminating in the preparation of this monograph.

We are especially honored that Harry Judge has written the foreword, providing a new marker, a decade and a half later, for his insightful and original Ford Foundation report, *American Graduate Schools of Education: A View from Abroad* (1982). Finally, we wish to thank David Imig, and the American Association of Colleges for Teacher Education, for their continuing leadership role in publishing this report.

We hold no one responsible but ourselves for the final formulations, but we know that this study is all the better for the many forms of assistance and ideas we received.

CHAPTER 1
THE PROBLEM

The past decade of reform in teacher education started with great fanfare in 1986 with the simultaneous publication of the Holmes Group's first report in the trilogy—*Tomorrow's Teachers*—and the Carnegie Forum's *A Nation Prepared: Teachers for the 21st Century*. In the same year, marking the occasion on a more ominous note, Seymour Sarason and his colleagues published a second edition of their 1962 book *The Preparation of Teachers: An Unstudied Problem in Education* (Sarason, Davidson, & Blatt, 1986), noting that the relationship between the preparation of teachers and the realities they experience in their careers is a question "as unstudied today—as superficially discussed today—as in previous decades" (p. xiv).

Especially for the Holmes Group, the next 5 years following 1986 was a period of great excitement, considerable debate, and activity concerning the reform of teacher education. This period encompassed the release of *Tomorrow's Schools* (1990), the second in the Holmes Group trilogy. Over the next 4 or 5 years, however, the intensity of the debate began to flag. The energy and enthusiasm of those working on the complex problems of implementing reform on the ground had been heavily taxed. During these years, the Holmes Group collective entered a phase of soul-searching, realizing that it was losing ground. In particular, the period 1993 to 1995 was one where we witnessed the loss of momentum. It was a time when the Holmes Group faced the question of what must be done to recapture and revitalize an agenda that had barely begun. By the time the third monograph—

Tomorrow's Schools of Education—was released in 1995, the initial momentum for reform had become more diffuse. Why do even the best of attempts fail? We will have recommendations in Chapter 3 to strengthen the Holmes efforts per se, but the problem is deeper than one group's effort. Society has failed its teachers in two senses of the word: it gives teachers failing grades for not producing better results; at the same time, it does not help improve the conditions that would make success possible.

Despite the rhetoric about teacher education in today's society, there does not seem to be a real belief or confidence that investing in teacher education will yield results. Perhaps deep down many leaders believe that teaching is not all that difficult. After all, most leaders have spent thousands of hours in the classroom and are at least armchair experts. And they know that scores of unqualified teachers are placed in classrooms every year and required to learn on the job. In addition, investing in teacher education is not a short-term strategy. With all the problems facing us demanding immediate solution, it is easy to overlook a preventative strategy that would take several years to have an impact. When a crisis occurs, you have to deal with it. A course of action that is aimed at preventing a crisis, despite being much less expensive in the mid to long term, is much harder to come by.

The problem begins with teacher preparation programs. Howey and Zimpher's (1989) detailed case studies of six universities in the United States enabled them to generate key attributes that would be necessary for program coherence, which they find lacking in existing programs, factors such as:

- programs based on clear conceptions of teaching and schooling;
- programs that have clear thematic qualities;
- faculty coalescing around experimental or alternative programs that have distinctive qualities;
- working with student cohort groups;
- adequate curriculum materials and a well-conceived laboratory component;

- articulation between on campus programming and field-based student teaching;
- direct linkage to research and development knowledge bases;
- regular program evaluation.

Goodlad (1990) and his associates in a comprehensive investigation of 29 universities are even more damning. Among their main findings:

1. The preparation programs in our sample made relatively little use of the peer socialization processes employed in some other fields of professional preparation. There were few efforts to organize incoming candidates into cohort groups or to do so at some later stage. Consequently, students' interactions about their experiences were confined for the most part to formal classes (where the teaching is heavily didactic). The social, intellectual, and professional isolation of teachers, so well described by Dan Lortie, begins in teacher education. This relatively isolated individualism in preparation seems ill-suited to developing the collegiality that will be demanded later in site-based school renewal.

2. The rapid expansion of higher education, together with unprecedented changes in academic life, have left professors confused over the mission of higher education and uncertain of their role in it. Although the effects of these changes in academic life transcend schools and departments, the decline of teaching in favor of research in most institutions of higher education has helped lower the status of teacher education. In regional public universities, once normal schools and teachers colleges, the situation has become so bad that covering up their historic focus on teacher education is virtually an institutional rite of passage. Teaching in the schools and teacher education seem unable to shake their condition of status deprivation.

3. There are serious disjunctures in teacher education programs: between the arts and sciences portion and that conducted in the school or department of education, from component to component of the so-called professional sequence, and between the campus-based portion and the school-based portion. . . . It is also clear from our data that the preparation underway in the programs we studied focused on *classrooms* but scarcely at all on *schools*.

4. Courses in the history, philosophy, and social foundation of education . . . have seriously eroded (pp. 700–701).

The beginning years of teaching do not fare any better. Induction programs to support beginning teachers are still very much in the minority, and good ones are rare, despite our very clear knowledge of the needs of beginning teachers, and despite the high probability that solid induction programs represent one of the most cost-efficient preventative strategies around.

The rest of the career isn't any more encouraging. From a learning point of view, the working conditions in most schools are not such that teachers become better by virtue of their work. Indeed, there is evidence that teachers even, and in some cases especially, the best ones become burnt out and cynical over their careers.

These problems and others are documented with resounding emphasis in the report of the National Commission on Teaching and America's Future (NCTAF). The commission found:

- In recent years, more than 50,000 people who lack the training required for their jobs have entered teaching annually on emergency or substandard licenses. [In 1990–1991, 27.4 percent of all newly hired teachers in the nation had no or substandard emergency licenses.]

- Nearly one-fourth (23 percent) of all secondary teachers do not have even a college minor in their main teaching field. This is true for more than 30 percent of mathematics teachers.

- Among teachers who teach a second subject, 36 percent are unlicensed in the field and 50 percent lack a minor.

- 56 percent of high school students taking physical science are taught by out-of-field teachers, as are 27 percent of those taking mathematics and 21 percent of those taking English. The proportions are much higher in high-poverty schools and in lower track classes.

- In schools with the highest minority enrollments, students have less than a 50 percent chance of getting a science or mathematics teacher who holds a license and a degree in the field he or she teaches. (1996, pp. 15–16)

The litany of problems, although familiar, is dramatically disturbing:

1. Low expectations for student performance;
2. Unenforced standards for teachers;
3. Major flaws in teacher preparation;
4. Painfully slipshod teacher recruitment;
5. Inadequate induction for beginning teachers;
6. Lack of professional development and rewards for knowledge and skill;
7. Schools that are structured for failure rather than success (NCTAF, 1996, p. 24).

As the commission argues, the problem is even more poignant. Many children, maybe as high as 50 percent of those disadvantaged, cannot assume that they will have "access to competent, caring, qualified teaching" (p. 21). In the absence of qualified, committed teachers, working very differently from the present, it is not possible to build an educational system that produces citizens essential for the kind of knowledge-based society that we now have. All Americans, argues the commission, have a critical interest in creating a system that "helps people to forge shared values, to understand and respect other perspectives, to learn and work at high levels of competence, to take risks and persevere against the odds, to work comfortably with people from diverse backgrounds, and to continue to learn through life" (p. 12).

In a related study we recently completed for the Rockefeller Foundation, assessing how four urban districts (Albuquerque, Flint, San Antonio, San Diego) could build professional development infrastructures to support the continuous development of educators, we noted three perennial problems:

1. The urban context: Community and parents
   Urban reform and school reform, to be successful, depend on each other. We agree that because many of the problems that plague city schools stem from the problems of the cities themselves, the full solution lies outside the schools as well as within them (Rury & Mirel, 1997). Some have gone so far as to say that it is pointless to work on school reform without prior community-building efforts (Mathews, 1996, p. 27). For us, this is not an either/or question. It is essential (among other strategies) to focus on school system infrastructure development, provided that this includes new relationships with communities.

   Analyzing the relationship between urban reform and school reform leads to the inevitable conclusion that professional development strategies, like building infrastructures, must be redefined to include more than teachers. Under conditions of poverty, including large discrepancies in living conditions across classes and races in cities, there can be little doubt that the mobilization of large numbers of caring adults is absolutely central to the chances of success. Therefore, building infrastructures strategies must explicitly encompass the development of, and relationships among, all those adults who can potentially affect the motivation, support, and learning of all students.

2. Fragmentation or coherence of reform initiatives

The Rockefeller *Building Infrastructures* initiative is only one of many reform initiatives underway in each of the four sites. As we shall show, however, the general problem is that these various projects not only are frequently unconnected, but also may work at cross purposes. At the very least, the existence of multiple initiatives often creates confusion in the minds of district educators, not to mention the public, as to how the reform strategies, taken as a whole, actually work. There is a great sense of fragmentation and lack of coherence in many urban districts engaged in reform. This is not just a matter of whether a few people can "explain" rational interrelationships of different reform strategies, but whether educators and others in the district experience and internalize a sense of clarity and direction.

3. Changing the teaching profession

The building infrastructures initiative is best seen in the larger context as part and parcel of a movement to determine whether the teaching profession itself will come of age. As the National Commission on Teaching and America's Future (1996) documents and argues, the teaching profession as a whole is badly in need of fundamental reform: in the recruitment, selection, and initial teacher education and induction to the profession; in the continuous professional development of educators; in the standards and incentives for professional work; and in the working conditions of teachers.

The fundamental problem with educational reform is that the teaching profession itself has not undergone the changes necessary to put it in the forefront of educational development (Fullan & Watson, 1997, pp. 6–7).

Reforms in teacher education, then, are part and parcel of changing the teaching profession itself, which in turn encompasses the redesign of the workplace—where and how teachers and students learn—which is intimately linked to parent and community reform. Changing the teaching force is the key to unlocking the forces required for systemic synergy.

In summary, the basic reason that most promising educational innovations fail is that schools are not organized for problem-solving, while teachers are not prepared for managing change and for taking the critical judgments and action steps to make them work. The current system is a dead horse. Flogging it with more innovations and demands can never be successful. There will always be lots of new ideas and innovations around in a knowledge society. We don't need more innovations; we need a greater capacity to deal with them. There is no pathway to this goal that does not involve the simultaneous renewal of teacher education and schools (as well as universities and communities).

We are, in brief, talking about what profound changes, hitherto unprecedented, in the teaching profession itself, and in its relationships to communities, universities, and other groups. Although the Holmes Group was to eventually conclude that it needed more allies and additional forces to accomplish the change needed, little did it know in 1985 that it was entering a period of work of such mammoth proportions.

CHAPTER 2
THE HOLMES GROUP: 1985–1995

The Holmes Group, a national consortium of nearly 100 research universities across the United States, has for the last 10 years consistently pushed for teacher education reform. The main mission of the Holmes Group is to make teacher education a central priority of the university by connecting it more closely to liberal arts education, to research on teaching and learning, and to practice in schools.

A Ford Foundation report published in 1982 had pointed to problems in the graduate schools of education at major research universities (Judge, 1982), essentially arguing that teacher education was a low priority in these institutions. The following year, a small group of education deans began to meet in what became the nucleus of the Holmes Group, named after Henry Holmes, dean of the Harvard Graduate School of Education in the 1920s. This original group, concluding that teacher education lacked both visibility and credibility, decided to focus on the twin themes of reform of teacher education and reform of the teaching profession. Their explicit goals included increased rigor for teacher preparation, improved standards of entry, recognition of differences in teachers' levels of knowledge and competence, improved relationships with schools, and improved conditions for professionals in schools.

The Ford Foundation, at the request of Holmes Group leaders themselves, commissioned us to conduct an external examination of the work of the Holmes Group in the context of reform in teacher education. The study was framed to address three overlapping questions:

- How appropriate were the goals and principles of the Holmes Group in relation to teacher education needs?
- What progress have member institutions made with the Holmes Group agenda?
- What impact has the Holmes Group had on the field of teacher education beyond its own member institutions?

Because the Holmes Group was only one of many forces influencing teacher education during the 1980s and 1990s, we opted for a wide-ranging inquiry into its work as part of a dynamic context of teacher education in the United States over the past decade. We tried to pull together disparate perspectives to provide reasoned conclusions about the Holmes Group and, at a more general level, to identify the problems and possibilities facing teacher education reform in the years ahead.

The study employed multiple forms of data gathering: literature and documents; a mailed survey questionnaire; interviews with key informants; and site visits. First, a summary of literature on the Holmes Group drew both on Holmes Group documents and on responses in published education literature. Second, survey questionnaires were sent to each Holmes Group member institution to obtain reports of changes in teacher education programs and support for the Holmes Group agenda. The survey was addressed to deans and a small selection of education faculty members (four in each institution) who had been involved with Holmes-related reform efforts. The response rate for the survey was just over 70 percent. Third, over 60 interviews were conducted nationally with key informants inside and outside the Holmes Group, all active in major education reform initiatives. Finally, two-day site visits were made to five schools of education in different regions of the country, all identified as making significant progress with the Holmes Group agenda. These were the University of Connecticut, Iowa State University, Louisiana State University, the University of Louisville, and the University of Utah. In each site, interviews were conducted with university faculty and personnel in professional development schools (PDSes).

The Holmes Group emerged at a time of great ferment about educational reform, both in the United States and in other countries. As reports such as *A Nation at Risk* pointed to what was seen by many as a crisis in American education, education scholars were also carrying out critical examinations of the conditions of schools (Boyer, 1983; Goodlad, 1984; Sizer, 1984). Although initial education reform efforts focused on schooling, soon the perspective broadened to include teaching and teacher education, with two influential reports published almost simultaneously in 1986: the Carnegie report, *A Nation Prepared: Teachers for the 21st Century* (Carnegie Forum on Education and the Economy, 1986) and the first report of the Holmes Group, *Tomorrow's Teachers.* These two set the terms of the debate about teacher preparation during the 1980s and beyond.

The Holmes Group, in bringing together leading American universities, created a critical mass with the potential of making major advances in the education of teachers. Several other organizations, however, also contributed to teacher education reform during the 1980s and 1990s. With such a plethora of actors, it is difficult to isolate the impact of any one group. John Goodlad and his colleagues, for instance, set forth their own recommendations for teacher education and established the National Network for Educational Renewal. Goodlad's proposals are most fully developed in his 1994 book, *Educational Renewal,* in which he details his vision of "centers of pedagogy" as a key to simultaneously improving both teacher education and schools. Project 30 Alliance, another reform group, was a consortium of teams of deans and leaders of education and of arts and sciences addressing the arts and sciences component of teacher education programs. The Renaissance Group, another university network, developed an agenda for reform that included some elements in common with the Holmes Group.

Nonetheless, the Holmes Group was a major player in the decade of reform launched in the mid-1980s. More than 100 research universities were invited to join [since 1986, 19 universities chose not to renew membership, and six new institutions (all historically Black colleges) joined].

We divide the rest of this chapter into three sections: an analysis of the Holmes Group's trilogy of publications, key findings in our study, and conclusions and recommendations.

A. THE TRILOGY

TOMORROW'S TEACHERS—LAUNCHING DEBATE AND REFORM

Tomorrow's Teachers, published in 1986, was the first major initiative of the Holmes Group. The report outlines proposals for the reform of teacher education in the form of five goals:

1. To make the education of teachers intellectually more solid.
2. To recognize differences in teachers' knowledge, skill, and commitment, in their education, certification, and work.
3. To create standards of entry to the profession—examinations and educational requirements—that are professionally relevant and intellectually defensible.
4. To connect our own institutions to schools.
5. To make schools better places for teachers to work and to learn (Holmes Group, 1986, p. 4).

Holmes Group leaders argued that the time had come for teaching to be considered a profession:

> The complexities of the educational enterprise are such that professionals are required. Professional preparation should include a liberal education, a subject matter major and minor, and introductory courses in education at the undergraduate level. (Case, Lanier, & Miskel, 1986, p. 42)

The report further argued that the teaching profession itself must be changed in order to reinforce changes in the content and standards of teacher education and provide preferential rewards to graduates of improved programs. Universities must join with schools to make schools better places for teachers and students.

Tomorrow's Teachers provoked intense interest and scrutiny in the educational community, eliciting both support and criticism. The *Teachers College Record,* for instance, devoted an entire issue to a symposium on the report's themes of the reform of teacher education and the continuing development of teaching as a profession. It is interesting to note that such a flurry of controversy did not accompany the second Holmes report, *Tomorrow's Schools,* published in 1990. Rather than introducing new issues, the second report developed more fully the plan for PDSes; subsequent discussion focused on implementation of a concept apparently supported by most in the education community. A third and final report completed the "Holmes trilogy." Long delayed, partly because of the difficulty of reaching internal consensus, *Tomorrow's Schools of Education* was finally published in mid-1995. In general, the reaction to this third report was one of disappointment rather than excitement (Gideonse, 1996; Labaree, 1995; Labaree & Pallas, 1996; Tyson, 1995). This report would turn out to be the least influential of the three.

Most education leaders acknowledged the need for a nationwide discussion of the problems associated with teacher education and schooling, with *Tomorrow's Teachers* regarded as a good starting point for such a dialogue. The Holmes Group was credited with recognizing the need for sweeping reform and providing leadership for it. Even those critical of the report noted its value in raising public awareness of long-standing teacher education issues. *Tomorrow's Teachers* received praise for its recognition of the close ties between the education system and social factors beyond the schools, as well as its acknowledgment that tinkering with teacher education programs would not be enough to bring about significant reform.

The reaction to the proposed agenda focused on two sets of issues: the five goals espoused in the report, and several themes neglected or otherwise seen as controversial.

The first three goals in the framework for teacher education reform were the subject of much debate. The remaining two goals were greeted with more acceptance, although issues around implementation were seen as somewhat problematic.

1. *To make the education of teachers intellectually more solid*

According to *Tomorrow's Teachers*, making the education of teachers intellectually more solid required significant changes in undergraduate education in the liberal arts and sciences, which would in turn shift the major portion of professional education for teachers to the graduate level. The proposals associated with this goal met with a great deal of debate, and indeed could be seen as having divisive effects on the teacher education community. Since previous attempts to reform the liberal arts curriculum had been unsuccessful, the Holmes Group was accused of naiveté in believing that their relatively powerless colleges of education would be able to make any substantial changes. In one sense, it might be argued that the Holmes Group bit off more than it could chew in making such broad and sweeping proposals. Although many schools and colleges of education in 1996 may have closer ties with arts and sciences than they did a decade earlier, there is little evidence of significant change in the substance or form of liberal arts studies.

The report did not establish any compelling rationale for requiring 4 years of liberal arts for all teachers, nor did it supply research data supporting the movement of teacher education to the postgraduate level. There have, however, been some studies suggesting that graduates of extended programs are more likely to enter teaching and more likely to stay in teaching than are graduates of four-year programs (Andrew, 1990; Andrew & Schwab, 1995). A review of the literature on extended teacher preparation programs, prepared for the National Commission on Teaching and America's Future, concludes that there is evidence of the benefits of extended programs in terms of placement and retention of new teachers, as well as teaching performance and professional commitment as perceived by graduates, principals and supervisors (Rustique & Darling-Hammond, 1996).

The Holmes Group was not the only professional body pushing for more rigor in teacher preparation. Throughout the 1980s, the National Council for the Accreditation of Teacher Education worked on improving the standards and procedures through which programs were accredited. The revised standards put a much stronger emphasis on the knowledge bases for professional education, although there was no explicit preference for graduate as opposed to undergraduate programs. Since the publication of *Tomorrow's Teachers*, the goal of making teacher education more intellectually knowledge-based remains, but the means of pursuing it include both graduate and undergraduate programs of varying length.

2. *To recognize differences in teachers' knowledge, skill, and commitment, in their education, certification, and work*

The Holmes Group, for the first time in higher education, proposed a career ladder for teachers. *Tomorrow's Teachers* proposed a framework that distinguished among:

- Instructors, individuals with undergraduate liberal arts degrees who were certified to teach for up to but not longer than 5 years, supervised closely by other professionals;
- Professional Teachers, people committed to teaching as a profession who have completed the necessary master's degree in teaching; and
- Career Professionals, whose "continued study and professional accomplishments" have earned them the

"highest license in teaching" (Holmes Group, 1986, p. 12).

Different roles and responsibilities would be assumed by teachers in the three categories.

Although a similar career ladder was also proposed by the Carnegie Forum report, neither the teacher education community nor the profession greeted the idea with enthusiasm. Available research suggests that career ladders, as they have been implemented, have been somewhat problematic, particularly when they are not part of larger reform efforts (Firestone, 1994). However, the idea of recognizing differences in teachers' skill and knowledge is receiving increased attention in various ways. The challenge is to develop systems that recognize the complexities of the work, encourage flexibility in schools and are acceptable to teachers. The National Board for Professional Teaching Standards (NBPTS, 1993) has developed a voluntary national system for recognizing the advanced professional expertise of teachers in both elementary and secondary schools. The system is being extended to cover most teaching specialties, has become increasingly accepted by teachers and their employers, and may be incorporated in future certification and licensing policies.

3. *To create standards of entry to the profession—examinations and educational requirements—that are professionally relevant and intellectually defensible*

Although agreeing that any profession must have standards for entry, commentators pointed out that there are weaknesses inherent in reform strategies that rely primarily on minimum standards, which are easily lowered when there is an overall teacher shortage or when there are vacancies in particular subject areas.

Tomorrow's Teachers was not, however, advocating simple entry-level exams. Holmes was breaking new ground by calling for serious development work in identifying and assessing the required knowledge base for teaching—a challenge taken up by several groups since 1987. The Educational Testing Service, for instance, has developed a new teacher assessment program, the PRAXIS® series, which includes academic skills assessments, subject assessments, and classroom performance assessment. Darling-Hammond and her colleagues (Darling-Hammond et al., 1995) document progress in developing appropriate standards for teacher licensure, as well as reviewing instruments for assessing teacher candidates. Many of these measures are performance-based rather than multiple-choice, paper-and-pencil tests. In addition to these professional testing programs, the Interstate New Teacher Assessment and Support Consortium (INTASC), operating under the auspices of the Council for Chief State School Officers, has articulated standards for initial licensing of teachers that are intended to be compatible with those of the National Board for Professional Teaching Standards. Ten states currently are piloting portfolio assessments for beginning teachers in several subject areas, based on INTASC standards.

4 and **5.** *Connecting universities to schools, and making schools better places for teachers to work and to learn*

There was little controversy about the remaining two goals: the difficulties came in establishing new institutional relationships and moving toward these goals.

The proposal for PDSes was enthusiastically received by many educators, both in universities and in schools. Involving schools in more cooperative arrangements was viewed as indicating that universities valued the practical and political skills of teachers. The proposal that universities become directly involved with public schools was seen as perhaps "the wisest long-term recommendation of the Holmes report" (Clements, 1987, p. 510).

As for the fifth goal of making schools better places for teachers, there was little disagreement about the desirability of such changes. However, there was doubt about whether the Holmes Group, a small group of research universities, would be able to influence significantly the working conditions in schools. A consortium involving only research universities would need allies. Later in our report, we discuss more fully the role of the Holmes Group in relation to the educational policy arena, but we note here that the Holmes Group postulated a reform agenda in areas that were beyond the control of universities operating on their own.

In addition to discussion of the five goals articulated in *Tomorrow's Teachers*, several other themes proved somewhat controversial.

THEMES

EQUITY AND DIVERSITY

Issues of equity and diversity were inadequately addressed in the first Holmes Group report, in that *Tomorrow's Teachers* paid little attention to the under-representation of minority teachers or to other equity concerns (Grant, 1990), nor did it address issues related to special education (Welch, 1993). The Holmes Group, quick to acknowledge that *Tomorrow's Teachers* had paid scant attention to these issues, acted to rectify the omission, primarily through two new initiatives. First, Holmes Group membership was expanded to include six historically Black colleges and universities. Second, an initiative called the Holmes Scholars program was established to provide recognition and support to outstanding minority graduate students in education and to encourage them to enter the education professoriate. We say more about this and other Holmes work around equity and diversity issues later in the report, when we discuss the Holmes Group as a national entity.

Considerable skepticism greeted the Holmes Group emphasis on the knowledge base of teaching and teacher education (Cornbleth, 1987; Jackson, 1987; Johnson, 1987; Labaree, 1992). Terms such as "knowledge base" and "micro and macro mechanisms that make schooling possible," were seen as conveying the impression that much of what prospective teachers must learn is technical and quasi-scientific. Even within the Holmes Group, however, there was uncertainty about knowledge claims. Judge (1987), a long-term adviser to the Holmes Group, cautioned against "overpressing" the view that the graduate schools of education have (or will have tomorrow) the knowledge base for teaching, suggesting that it is power and autonomy, more than knowledge, that link the historic professions to the universities. While arguing that we are considerably more informed than we were about the scientific base informing both teaching and teacher preparation, Howey (1990) too, acknowledged that "we still have much to learn" (p. 4). In fact, as we shall see, research on teacher education, even in the PDS, remains woefully underdeveloped.

VALUES AND GOALS OF EDUCATION

To many educators, the stress on knowledge and technical competence inadequately addressed questions about values, such as the "three Cs of care, concern, and connection" in teacher education (Martin, 1987, p. 408). This "moral dimension" of education and of teacher education has been a focus of the work of Goodlad and his colleagues (Goodlad, 1994). The Holmes Group soon responded to such concerns. The second Holmes Group report, *Tomorrow's Schools*, with its emphasis on including "everybody's children," "resonates with concern about promoting greater social opportunity and personal empowerment for students and teachers alike" (Labaree, 1992, p. 145).

SUMMARY COMMENT ON TOMORROW'S TEACHERS AND THE EMERGENCE OF HOLMES

The publication of *Tomorrow's Teachers* was a catalyst for much-needed discussion and dialogue around the issues of teacher education and the reform of teaching itself. Perhaps the most significant aspect of the report was its timeliness: just as questions and concerns were arising about teacher education and its role in education reform, *Tomorrow's Teachers* provided an agenda for debate and action. Coming from such an influential group, the report received wide publicity and careful reading. *Tomorrow's Teachers* articulated many of the critical issues that shaped and fed into the reform initiatives in teacher education since 1986. The publication set in motion an excitement that infused the next 5 years of activity.

A TIME OF TRANSITION

Even before the publication of the second report in 1990, shifts could be observed in the emphasis given to the goals set out in the first report. In 1988, Lanier and Featherstone, writing on behalf of the Holmes Group, provided a progress report in which they stressed as important the creation of PDS and the recruitment of minority teachers. Although continuing to suggest that the undergraduate degree in education be replaced with a major in the arts, they acknowledged that within Holmes institutions a variety of programs and degree structures existed which were described as "suited to diverse institutional needs" (p. 21). The earlier insistence on extended programs seemed to be moderating somewhat. A later analysis of reform efforts revealed considerable variation in the length and type of program offered; some 4-year, some extended 5-year, and some postbaccalaureate (Yinger & Hendricks, 1990).

TOMORROW'S SCHOOLS—PROFESSIONAL DEVELOPMENT SCHOOLS (PDS)

With the publication in 1990 of the second report, *Tomorrow's Schools*, the Holmes Group outlined in more detail its plan for "connecting schools of education with schools" (Goal 4 of *Tomorrow's Teachers*), largely through the Professional Development School. The "goals" of the first report became "principles" in the second report, indicating, perhaps, a renewed understanding of the difficulties faced in prescribing courses of action. In this second report, teachers seemed to be viewed as partners in reform and potential colleagues in educational research.

As outlined in the report, the six principles for the design of PDSes were as follows:

1. Teaching and learning for understanding;
2. Creating a learning community;
3. Teaching and learning for understanding for everybody's children;
4. Continuing learning by teachers, teacher educators, and administrators;
5. Thoughtful, long-term inquiry into teaching and learning;
6. Inventing a new institution (The Holmes Group, 1990, p. 7).

These principles, according to the report, are offered as "starting points for conversations and negotiations among university and school faculties embarked on a mutual endeavor" (p. 6). Although the principles were not "heavily prescriptive," neither were they "lightly held" (ibid.). There is a definite recognition here that "a template for a single conception" (p. 6) was inadequate for the task at hand. In PDSes, practicing teachers and administrators come together with university faculty in partnerships to improve teaching and learning for their respective students. The professional development school is to be a center of responsible innovation where new programs and technologies can be tried out and evaluated.

The concept of the professional development school or clinical practice school did not originate with the Holmes Group. In addition to laboratory schools at many universities, considerable experience had

been gained during the 1970s and early 1980s, for instance in Jefferson County, Kentucky (Schlechty & Joslin, 1984; Whitford & Hovda, 1986) and Salt Lake City, Utah (Nutting, 1985). Several deans active in the early Holmes Group brought with them what had been learned through this work. But Holmes, we believe, was the first group to articulate and focus on PDSes starting with Goal 4 in *Tomorrow's Teachers* and intensifying its efforts in *Tomorrow's Schools*.

What conditions must be met for a school to be a professional development school has been an matter of long-standing debate in the Holmes Group and elsewhere: some insist that PDSes, in order to be eligible for the label, must meet a number of defined standards, while others are more flexible. One dean interviewed in our study went so far as to suggest that a professional development school is "whatever you can achieve. You can't control and be precise; schools aren't like this." A different view was expressed by Murray (1993) who outlined what he termed "all or none" criteria for PDSes. In yet another view, "the professional development school is best thought of as an ideal type toward which reform-minded schools are striving" (Nystrand, 1991, p. 1).

PDSes form a cornerstone of the Holmes Group's work, and for that reason we will examine them more closely in our discussion of findings.

THE NEXT STAGE OF REFORM: TOMORROW'S SCHOOLS OF EDUCATION

The final report in the Holmes Group trilogy, *Tomorrow's Schools of Education,* was the product of a long and difficult gestation period. A scan of several issues of the *Holmes Group Forum* provides clues about the process of developing what was, in effect, intended to be a grand design for colleges of education for the 21st century. Originally scheduled for release in 1993, the report was delayed several times and was finally published in summer 1995. The report tackles the problem of uneven quality in the preparation and selection of educators. Since the quality of teachers is tied to the quality of their preparation, teacher education cannot be improved without changing the places where teachers are prepared. Focusing on why and how schools of education must redefine and reorganize themselves to meet new needs, the report proposes a set of characteristics that would define a high-quality professional school of education, and lists a series of "action steps" to raise standards. The Holmes action agenda has now broadened to include all colleges that prepare teachers. Addressing the uneven quality of programs offered by teacher education institutions, *Tomorrow's Schools of Education* suggests that colleges not prepared to raise quality should get out of the business.

The report, a somewhat polemical document, created considerable controversy within the Holmes Group, and had to be revised several times before its final publication to meet the concerns of member institutions. However, it has generated relatively little professional or public reaction. Tyson (1995) called the report "a curious mixture of scathing self-criticism, high ideals, revolutionary talk, timid reform proposals, and stunning omissions" (p. 3), and went on to conclude:

> There are many true and good ideas in *Tomorrow's Schools of Education,* and certainly the Holmes Group should be credited with bold self-examination and a measured step toward profession building. But it seems to be caught midway between its old

view of itself as the elite cadre that spreads excellence over the landscape and its new view of itself as the servant of practitioners and the children they serve. (p. 6)

The document contains a number of "big ideas" in its agenda for reforming schools, colleges, and departments of education. First, knowledge development is to be linked to clients and users, primarily through PDSes. Second, serious and substantial ongoing professional development is seen as critical for all those involved in education. Third, schools of education are to be active in policy development. Fourth, diversity is to be a key goal, among faculty, students, and PDSes.

Tomorrow's Schools of Education does appropriately up the ante for the establishment of PDSes by emphasizing three basic commitments: "professional learning in the context of sound practice," "improvement-oriented inquiry," and "education standard setting," all of which we would agree are critical if PDSes are to fulfill their potential. We also agree with *Tomorrow's Schools of Education's* view that PDSes should not be just another project (although in many cases they are just that), but must become integral to the institutional life of a school of education.

While agreeing that the PDS must be a central component of the reform strategy, we find that *Tomorrow's Schools of Education* appears to have neglected other vital elements in the "simultaneous renewal" proposition.

First, and curiously in light of its title, the report fails to address *the transformation of universities and schools of education*. This is doubly ironic because *Tomorrow's Schools of Education* takes universities to task for their failure to create PDSes, but then does not take up the corresponding agenda of how to transform and build on the strengths of the universities. The report does speak to collective will, a critical mass of faculty, incentives, and staffing, but far more attention is given to inventing PDSes—the school side of the equation—than to inventing new schools of education. As many reform-oriented schools of education are finding, restructuring and reculturing higher education requires an intensive focus in its own right, largely because universities are used to studying others, not themselves (Fullan, 1998). As observed by Gideonse (1996), the report "says virtually nothing about tomorrow's schools of education as structures or institutions, although it offers exciting glimpses of activities, curricula, and processes that might be observed in a school of education modeling what is known about learning" (p. 150).

Second, although *Tomorrow's Teachers* put considerable emphasis on strengthening connections with the rest of the university and ensuring that prospective teachers have more rigorous preparation in the arts and sciences, *Tomorrow's Schools of Education* suggested few specific proposals for strengthening the relationship to the arts and sciences, beyond insisting on the importance of doing so.

WE FEAR THAT TOO MUCH FREIGHT IS BEING PLACED ON THE PDS.

Third, while the Holmes Group has continually referred to the education of educators, there is a tendency to slip into focusing on the initial preparation of teachers. Reform must address the education of *all* professionals, not just beginning teachers—administrators, counselors, and psychologists, advanced teachers, professors of education, and so on—a point stressed by Harry Judge in the foreword to this book, and also emphasized by Labaree (1995). Although the report does acknowledge the importance of these professionals, tomorrow's schools of education are portrayed as primarily places devoted to the preparation and support of teachers.

Fourth, we fear that too much freight is being placed on the PDS. If PDSes represent islands of improvement, how do we "make islands into archipelagoes" (Hargreaves, 1995) and make the PDS part of a larger school reform effort? Further, in its enthusiasm for professional development school research, *Tomorrow's Schools of Education* could be read as suggesting that the PDS is "the only acceptable subject and site for education school research" (Labaree, 1995, p. 194).

In 1995, the Holmes Group began a process to change its structure and membership, indeed its very strategy, as it concluded that more allies were needed. Instead of an organization restricted to a relatively small number of research universities, the group began to expand and establish new alliances. An enlarged Board of Directors, with representatives from professional education organizations, schools, and school districts, met throughout the year to draw up recommendations about organizational aims, membership, structure, leadership, and priorities. Membership in the new organization will include professional organizations in education, as well as partnerships between research universities and school districts and other institutions that prepare teachers. We return to these new developments in Chapter 3.

B. KEY FINDINGS

We have organized the findings around three levels of activity: first, the Holmes Group in local contexts; second, the Holmes Group as a national entity; and third, the Holmes Group in the broader policy context of teacher education reform.

I. THE HOLMES GROUP IN LOCAL CONTEXTS

Tomorrow's Teachers, in addition to initiating national debate about teacher education reform, also provided a catalyst for local action. In the mid 1980s, and at a time when teacher education was being left out of the equation of school reform, *Tomorrow's Teachers* appeared, quickly placing teacher education in the middle of the equation. The action was not restricted to Holmes member universities, but was characteristic of many teacher education institutions. Intense discussion about the Holmes and Carnegie reports was accompanied by a surge of enthusiastic reform activity in colleges of education and in many K–12 schools associated with these colleges. The goal of making teaching a profession through graduate preparation and research-based programs appealed to many in higher education, but understandably more to those in research universities than in colleges with only undergraduate programs.

Membership in the Holmes Group was seen by many universities to be highly desirable. Indeed, some colleges of education seemed to enjoy a much-needed boost in status because of their new prestigious association. The Holmes Group provided a platform and an agenda that could be used as leverage within the university to facilitate teacher education reform. In the words of one dean who had used Holmes membership to advantage, "Holmes came along at a good time. Joining gave external validation and impetus to do things that we considered to be the right things."

It is important to note that because our site visits were all to schools or colleges of education seen as making good progress with the Holmes agenda, they gave a restricted picture of teacher education reform. In all cases, Holmes had significantly impacted the local scene. The Holmes Group occasionally provided almost a template for program change—for instance at Louisiana State University—but more often the Holmes agenda gave additional impetus to changes that were already underway, or at least anticipated by the dean and a few key faculty members. This was the case, for instance, at the University of Connecticut, the University of Louisville, and the University of Utah. For other institutions, such as Iowa State University, the Holmes Group operated to "kick-start" a process of rethinking structure and program, but beyond providing direction and some common language, seemed to have only a moderate influence on the specifics of the new programs that evolved.

Our survey and interview data uncovered a number of themes related to initial local membership and local action. Each of these is discussed in the following section on local campus activity of member institutions.

PROGRAM REDESIGN

If any Holmes Group initiative caught the attention of teacher educators nationally, it was the call for extended and/or graduate teacher preparation programs. Our data suggest that local conditions and state policy contexts often limited efforts to implement this agenda item. In the survey, less than half of the deans reported that their colleges had moved to extended programs. Financial and political considerations were paramount for many institutions, but the absence of empirical data supporting a shift to extended programs was also cited as a reason for maintaining the undergraduate program. In some cases, 5th-year programs were started, only to see a return to undergraduate teacher education, usually due to declines in enrollment. It seems that for further progress to be made, policy and licensing systems would have to be developed to reinforce extended programs—without such contextual supports, many universities will find it difficult to maintain longer and thus more expensive programs.

An aspect of program redesign that came to the fore with the publication of *Tomorrow's Schools* was the need to prepare teachers to work with all children to meet the needs of learners in an increasingly diverse society. In our surveys, deans and faculty members were asked the degree to which their programs addressed teacher education in these important areas. Although 60–70 percent of the deans and faculty members reported that their teachers are moderately-to-well prepared to attend to the issues of race, culture, gender, and class, less than 20 percent of respondents actually claim their students are "well-prepared" to address these issues. Nonetheless, these data are consistent with the data gathered by the AACTE Research About Teacher Education Project, suggesting that nationally most deans and faculty believe that they are working on the problem of preparing teachers to work in diverse settings, although very little performance-based data are available to indicate the success of such programs.

Deans and faculty were also asked about other areas that were part of the Holmes reform agenda. Program redesign appears to be marked by a "broken front," with change in some areas outstripping that in others. Reports from deans were consistently more positive than those from faculty members. Areas in which the most progress was reported were a conceptual framework to guide the program, more rigorous standards of entry into teacher education programs, and improved assessments for preservice teacher candidates. Areas in which least progress was reported were: articulating learning goals for student teachers, making inquiry integral to the teacher preparation program, and evaluating teacher education programs.

When asked about the impetus for reform in their school or college of education, about 40 percent of the respondents attribute the changes made so far to participation in the Holmes Group. It is interesting to note that the few deans at the institutions that are members of both Holmes and of the National Network for Educational Renewal (NNER) could not trace the historical roots of the many actions they and the faculty have taken to achieve renewal of the teacher education programs, because the agendas are similar. Teacher education reform at these sites is not identified as either Holmes or NNER; it is reform, first and foremost.

The local data, as gained by the surveys and the site visits, suggest initial progress but limited systematic development in the redesign of teacher education programs. This is the source of the fragility that seems associated with reform in preservice programs. To bring about reforms in teacher education, a set of variables must come together. The leadership must be visible, stable, and strong. The faculty must buy into and own the agenda. The norms of the academy must be made malleable to achieve curricular flexibility. Local schools must accept the rationale and the new programs to provide the types of field experiences necessary to prepare teachers for classroom practice. As if these four broad areas don't present enough of a challenge, each must also be balanced against the others. In many ways, it is remarkable that some of the Holmes initiatives have taken hold at some member institutions, particularly in the absence of explicit strategies for linking local action with the national agenda.

RELATIONSHIPS WITH SCHOOLS

The Holmes Group has been a strong proponent of colleges of education developing stronger ties to local schools, and it is clear

SITE VISITS OFFERED A MORE NUANCED PICTURE OF FIELD DEVELOPMENT.

from our data that progress is being made on this agenda. Three-quarters of our survey respondents report that they have been assisting schools in school improvement efforts and that teachers are participating in the changes being made in the preservice programs. However, the site visits offered a more nuanced picture of field development. Even in these sites, seen as making good progress with the Holmes agenda, program redesign did not seem to be characterized by strong local teacher participation. In all sites, school personnel had been involved in early discussions about teacher education reform and establishment of PDSes. However, once PDSes were operating and initial changes had been made, curriculum still seemed to be the proprietary interest of the university faculty. Although school leaders were kept apprised of the changes occurring, school personnel were not always active in the design of the courses and programs.

In reconciling our conclusions from the site visits with the survey data, it appears that there may be considerable involvement of field personnel with various aspects of the teacher preparation programs, but decision-making about such programs seems to belong to the university rather than the field.

PROFESSIONAL DEVELOPMENT SCHOOLS (PDS)

If any aspect of the Holmes agenda has shown signs of enduring, it is the expectation that member institutions will conduct teacher education in PDSes. A commitment to establish PDSes was a requirement for membership (The Holmes Group, 1986, p. 66). Some Holmes Group members had already established collaborative relationships with school districts and others quickly followed. The PDS initiative had soon spread across the teacher education community. Colleges of education with a history of collaboration with the field saw PDSes as consistent with their earlier work and intensified their activities, while others initiated new projects. We look closely at PDSes because they are so central to the Holmes agenda, and so complex as a change strategy.

By 1995, according to our survey data, all responding Holmes institutions reported at least one professional development school. The apparent universality of PDSes, however, should be interpreted in light of Gehrke's observation that many colleges display a "trophy mentality" about PDSes (Gehrke, 1991); in other words, what counts is having one. The extent to which a professional development school actually exemplifies the characteristics outlined in *Tomorrow's Schools* is difficult to determine, but many of our interviews suggested that the gap between rhetoric and reality is wide.

While the survey data suggest that the PDS may be the Holmes reform dimension that lasts, our site visits suggest that the PDSes that exist are not yet "continuous improvement" schools peopled by teachers, preservice teachers, and university faculty. Those who have worked to develop PDSes agree with those who have written about them that difficulties abound.

Resources have been a challenge, since establishing PDSes can be costly. A Michigan partnership (involving business, government, and universities), established to improve education, provided several million dollars to set up and support PDS (Holmes Group Forum, Winter 1990). On the other hand, the majority of PDSes appear to have been developed with few extra financial resources. For example, in the five colleges of education portrayed in the case profiles for this study, most PDSes were operated from general revenues, on a basis not significantly different from that of other schools. In some sites, university faculty members spent significant amounts of time in the schools on a regular basis. In such cases, their contribution provided additional resources and flexibility, as did the time of teaching interns, who were usually expert enough to take on substantial school responsibilities. The University of Louisville and the Jefferson County Schools provided modest funding to encourage new and creative initiatives that would otherwise be difficult to launch, and found that small amounts of money can have a significant impact.

Collaboration between schools and faculties of education is another challenge. Data from our respondents support Nystrand's (1991) observation about the differences in organizational culture between schools and universities. Differences include varying approaches to work roles, reward systems, and organizational structures. However, universities and schools are similar in having crowded schedules and little time to embark on new initiatives. If PDSes are to be successful, commitment and involvement is required from the top (deans and superintendents) and from the grass roots (teachers and faculty members). The Holmes Group has stressed the interconnectedness of schools and universities, acknowledging the need for what Goodlad has referred to as "simultaneous renewal" of K–12 schools and teacher education programs. Our data suggest that PDSes, valuable as they are, are on their own an insufficient strategy for changing two such complex social institutions.

Clinical faculty are often appointed to take on the main responsibility for PDS programs. However, it might be argued, these staff are neither fish nor fowl. They are not teachers, nor do they enjoy the usual rights and privileges of university faculty, since they are rarely eligible for tenure-track positions. They are school-based teacher educators who are not expected to conduct research, but may be expected to lead local teachers in action research. They might be essential, but might also be keeping university faculty and PDS teachers at arms-length from one another. Given the importance of scholarship in the leading research universities, it is somewhat ironic that basing so much of teacher preparation in PDSes has sometimes meant that research faculty are less involved. The labor-intensive work of PDSes may lead research faculty to decrease their involvement, a decision made possible by the presence of clinical faculty to pick up the load. Regardless of the infusion of "inquiry" throughout the teacher preparation program, without the strong participation of research faculty members, teacher preparation in PDS sites may emphasize practice and clinical work at the expense of scholarship.

It is the *research* goal of PDSes that raises the most fundamental questions and limitations of this strategy. PDSes were supposed to help the teaching profession in six fundamental ways:

1. By promoting much more ambitious conceptions of teaching and learning on the part of prospective teachers in universities and students in schools.

2. By adding to and reorganizing the collections of knowledge we have about teaching and learning.

3. By ensuring that enterprising, relevant, responsible research and development is done in schools.

4. By linking experienced teachers' efforts to renew their knowledge and advance their status with efforts to improve their schools and to prepare new teachers.

5. By creating incentives for faculties in the public schools and faculties in the education schools to work mutually.

6. By strengthening the relationship between schools and the broader political, social, and economic communities in which they reside (Holmes Group, 1990, pp. 1–2).

We found little evidence of progress of research in PDSes. Much of the formal inquiry in the PDS sites we visited was being conducted by teacher interns as part of the requirements of their programs. In other cases, teachers were involved in action research related to a university course or graduate program. As Howey (1996) notes about PDSes in general, larger programs of research are "all but absent at the present time across and within the vast majority of PDSes" (p. 181).

There is some indication that teachers and principals in PDSes were enthused about their participation, and were perhaps more involved in professional development as a result, but it appears that the impact of this work remains undocumented and thus permanently lost.

A further problem relates to the values and incentives for scholarship in higher education. In our interviews, we often hear that untenured faculty members felt the need to disengage from

PDSes to make time for more of the kind of research and writing that would be recognized for tenure and promotion. The theory is that faculty working in close partnership with teachers in PDSes will in the long run achieve greater school improvement, better teacher education for all concerned, greater integration of theory and practice, and more grounded and valid research. But as Judge, Carriedo, & Johnson (1995) observe:

> There is much in the culture of higher education itself which ensures that these longer term gains are nearly always less persuasive than the shorter term pressures on faculty, and especially on junior faculty. (p. 11)

Stated another way, the broader institutional conditions and support required to assist a serious program of research are not yet established.

Finally, what about PDSes as a strategy for school improvement? Is the development of such prototypes a productive strategy for teacher education and school reform? We have already seen one problem: either conditions for development may not exist, or the conditions for documenting the results may be weak. A second issue relates to whether networks are set up for PDSes to learn from each other. By far the most serious shortfall, however, is the assumption that PDSes will influence other schools in the district and beyond. The vision is that PDSes would be networked or otherwise influence non-PDSes. We don't blame the Holmes Group when we conclude that "they don't exert such influence."

Andy Hargreaves (1996), in the American Educational Research Association symposium on our report, discussed it this way:

> What is teacher preparation a route to? The goal is not to create a high quality program as an end in itself, but rather to influence the sustained quality of teaching and learning in schools over time, across systems. Teacher education should be a subsidiary question to the larger one of improvement of systems. Conceptually you may create excellent candidates who are doomed to die on the rocks of untransformed schools.

Hargreaves goes on to talk about the wider institutional problem. PDSes are projects rather than new institutional ways of life. They can be marginalized by creating small enclaves (Hargreaves calls them "Epcot Centers") of activity unconnected with the rest of the district. He concludes by arguing that the starting point should not begin with teacher preparation or PDSes, but with the question of what role should schools of education play in wider systemic change.

We do not dwell on the PDS to criticize Holmes, but rather to argue that a much more comprehensive strategy is needed to accomplish the goals set out—one that is beyond the grasp of the Holmes Group working alone.

STATE CONTEXT

Because schools, colleges, and departments of education are inevitably affected by the context in which they operate, local reform is inevitably influenced by state policies and practices. Requiring a master's degree for teacher certification, for instance, may be a requirement easier to sustain in a state with high teacher salaries than in a state with low teacher salaries. In some states, teacher licensing policies entail rigorous standards, supporting those colleges of education with extended programs and high entry qualifications. In other states, "such initiatives are undermined by the resurgence of licensing practices aimed at putting teachers in classrooms quickly and cheaply" (Darling-Hammond & Goodwin, 1993, p. 35) through quick alternative certification programs. In some states, such as South Carolina, policy frameworks have been approved to provide funding for PDSes (Ishler & Edens, undated), with clearly articulated criteria concerning how universities and schools would qualify for funding. We would venture to say that at the time the Holmes Group was operating, state policy was inimical to the goals set out in the trilogy.

In brief, state policy remains a powerful variable which can impede or assist local development. The comprehensive goals of the education of all educators, and the simultaneous renewal of universities and schools, are not likely to be achieved without a supportive policy context, a matter we return to in Chapter 3.

II. THE HOLMES GROUP AS A NATIONAL ENTITY

Given the plethora of actors in teacher education during the last decade, disentangling the role and impact of the Holmes Group as compared to that of other events or groups is difficult if not impossible. Some of these other developments include the work of the National Board for Professional Teaching Standards; the Interstate New Teacher Assessment and Support Consortium, operating under the auspices of the Council for Chief State School Officers; new standards for the National Council for the Accreditation of Teacher Education; John Goodlad's National Network for Educational Renewal; and the emergence of other networks and consortia such as the Renaissance Group, Project 30 Alliance, and the Urban Network for Improving Teacher Education. Nonetheless, we are confident in concluding that the Holmes Group had a substantial effect on teacher education reform at the national level, within regions and states, and in many individual schools, colleges, and departments of education.

At the national level, the Holmes Group set the terms of the debate, focused the discussion, and served as the catalyst for much of the change that occurred. Even for those critical of the proposed changes, the Holmes Group shaped much of the teacher education reform agenda in the mid-to-late 1980s. The Holmes Group went beyond producing an agenda for action; the simultaneous formation of a consortium of nearly 100 major universities, all devoted to improving teacher education, also provided a forum in which to implement the agenda. The Holmes Group was not an outside group recommending changes to education, but was rather a group of insiders committing to a new agenda.

The impact of the Holmes Group was enhanced by several factors, some having to do with the agenda itself, and others having more to do with extraneous forces. That the message of *To-*

morrow's Teachers was similar in many ways to that of the Carnegie Forum report, *A Nation Prepared*, strengthened the overall impact. At least at the beginning of its life, the Holmes Group agenda was seen as relatively clear: longer and more intellectually rigorous teacher preparation programs and improved clinical preparation for teachers through PDSes. Although not simple, the agenda was coherent, and if implemented, it promised not only better programs and better prepared teachers, but also greater influence for teacher educators. Much of what was new in the 1986 reports of both the Holmes Group and the Carnegie Forum has now become part of what is commonly accepted as a desirable direction for reform, although it may not yet be visible in many schools and colleges of education.

The timing of the Holmes Group was another important factor in its early success. The Holmes Group appeared in the reform arena at a critical point in the history of teacher education, just as the first wave of American educational reform was giving way to the second. As reformers moved to consider more complex proposals to restructure schools, it became clear that radical changes would be required in the work and the training of teachers. Most of the agenda for proceeding with this difficult task was provided by the Holmes Group, with the publication of *Tomorrow's Teachers*.

Five themes emerged from our data concerning the Holmes Group as a national entity—prestige, focus and momentum, equity/diversity, ideas versus action, and organizational issues.

PRESTIGE

The much vaunted "prestige" of the Holmes Group has been a double-edged sword throughout the decade of its life. There is no doubt that the prestige of a group whose membership included leading American universities lent credibility to its suggested reforms. As well, the prospect of being in such company was certainly influential in persuading many universities to join. As noted earlier in the report, many deans were able to take advantage of this perceived status boost to move the reform agenda forward more rapidly than would otherwise have been possible. To the extent that prestige was associated with high-quality programs and progress in improving teacher education, it was a positive force. On the other hand, an air of exclusionary elitism was associated with the Holmes Group. Of the 250 institutions offering doctoral degrees in education, less than half were invited to join the Holmes Group, a situation that created some resentment. Such resentment increased as it became clear that not all Holmes members were committed to acting on the Holmes agenda for reform, while many non-Holmes institutions were working hard to improve their teacher preparation programs and establish PDS. For some of the most prestigious research universities, although they often continued as nominal Holmes members, reforming teacher education was not a high priority. At a national level, the Holmes leadership was in the awkward position of advocating an agenda not being pursued by some of its most powerful member institutions.

The challenge for the future is to ensure that prestige is associated with strong, high-quality programs, rather than with belonging to a group that could be seen as exclusionary.

FOCUS AND MOMENTUM

During the early years, the agenda of the Holmes Group was seen as relatively clear. Holmes stood for higher standards, extended programs of teacher preparation, closer ties with arts and sciences, and PDSes. However, the distinction between accepting a set of goals and actually implementing them soon became apparent, and one dean suggested that the early consensus might be more accurately described as "false clarity." Many schools of education, as they considered the pros and cons of moving to graduate-level certification programs, decided that the contexts in which they operated would not support such a move. Many schools of education also had less success than expected in coordinating their efforts with their colleagues in the arts and sciences.

The Holmes Group also had problems addressing two of its more ambitious goals—goals which the whole field has failed to deal with. One concerned the preparation and roles of other professionals in addition to teachers—psychologists, social workers, other health professionals, and administrators. The other involves linkages to parents and the community. *Tomorrow's Schools*, it will be recalled, was concerned to strengthen "the relationship between schools and the broader political, social, and economic communities in which they reside" (1990, p. 2). The question of focus—how limited and how comprehensive—occupied much of the debate surrounding the drafting of *Tomorrow's Schools of Education.*

Related to questions of focus is loss of momentum. The Holmes Group started with a great surge of energy and excitement. The first major report, *Tomorrow's Teachers*, stimulated widespread and lively debate in the literature, on university campuses, and at professional and academic meetings. The teacher education community, at least that part of it involved with research universities, became engaged in a process of rethinking what they were about and grappling with how to change their programs and their relationships with the field.

WE BELIEVE THAT THE LOSS OF MOMENTUM WAS RELATED TO . . . A LOSS OF FOCUS [AND] . . . THE MAGNITUDE OF THE WORK.

After initially capturing the marketplace of ideas, however, the evidence from the multiple data sources tapped in this study indicate that the Holmes Group began to lose momentum, particularly in the last 5 years. *Tomorrow's Schools* came out after the publication of *Tomorrow's Teachers*; it was another 5 years before the appearance of *Tomorrow's Schools of Education.* During the latter 5-year period, the Holmes Group seemed preoccupied with its own future, allowing other actors to take over the reform agenda. By the time *Tomorrow's Schools of Education* finally appeared, many readers were disappointed to find what they saw as bromides and "polemical prose" that provided little concrete help in reforming schools of education and seemed to underplay crucial components of the reform agenda.

What contributed to the loss of momentum? Judith Lanier (1996) claimed in the AERA symposium that it was related to the fact that the "real work" had begun in the 1990s. The early work in the late 1980s, she notes, was merely talk. The actual doing of it proved to be extremely difficult. Consistent with this, we believe that the loss of momentum was related to two major interacting factors. First, there was a loss of focus, as people realized that everything related to everything else, and debates resulted in further confusion or frustration. Second, the magnitude of the work was such that it simply could not be done by these institutions working by themselves. It required a much larger combination of forces.

EQUITY AND DIVERSITY

After a slow start in relation to issues of equity and diversity, the organization has made significant progress on some dimensions of equity The Holmes Group leadership was quick to acknowledge the earlier omission of equity and diversity issues, initiating several actions that indicated a new commitment to diversity. First, six historically Black colleges and universities, the institutions that prepare the largest number of teachers from minority backgrounds, became full members of the Holmes Group. In recognition of their limited financial resources, the Holmes Board has provided small grants to facilitate their participation in the consortium. Although the six institutions have been involved in varying degrees, in at least some colleges membership has been influential in helping deans and faculty to reform and further strengthen their teacher preparation programs.

The second initiative was the establishment of the Holmes Scholars program to identify and support promising minority graduate students in education, a program that allowed the Holmes Group to make real progress with addressing diversity. The intent of the program was to help create a pool of competent, qualified scholars of color, as well as scholars with disabilities. The program was seen as benefiting higher education by increasing the pool of potential faculty members from diverse backgrounds by providing financial support, mentoring, and recognition as the Holmes Scholars proceeded through their doctoral programs and sought academic positions.

With over 100 Holmes Scholars, the program is an exception to a frequently reported perception of the Holmes Group as concerned more with words than action. Holmes Scholars themselves are very positive about the program and the benefits to their studies and careers. Networking and mutual support among the Holmes Scholars has been a major strength of the program. For many young scholars, accustomed to being the only or one of very few students of color, it is "affirming and exhilarating to be in a room with 50 or 60 other people all engaged in doctoral studies." A challenge for the future is to provide more guidance to schools, colleges, and departments of education as to how ensure better mentoring and guidance to Holmes Scholars for successfully beginning and building an academic career. Another difficulty has been the scarcity of available tenure track positions in the university marketplace over the past few years. Several interviewees stressed the need to encourage schools and colleges of education to look to the Holmes Scholars program as a source of new faculty.

Overall, both Holmes Scholars and others agree this program has been highly successful and must be continued regardless of the future of the Holmes Group. One dean who had hired several former Holmes Scholars noted that all the faculty at the school of education "now put a higher priority on recruiting minorities." The presence of several young faculty of color had increased the level of awareness among all faculty members.

In her evaluation of Holmes Group equity and diversity initiatives, Irvine (1994) emphasized that the curriculum and preparation of all student teachers has to change if all teachers are to be able to instruct children of color. Since the PDSes did not go very far in developing and documenting new teacher education curriculum more generally, as we have seen, it is not surprising that PDSes as prototypes of equity-based reform are not in evidence.

Valli, Cooper, and Frankes (1996, p. 263) in a comprehensive review of research on equity in PDSes, confirm this conclusion in observing that "we are still a long way from knowing whether PDSes can do better than other schools in terms of disentangling social class inequalities from learning opportunities" (Holmes Group, 1990, p. 34).

The Holmes Group, especially in its latter two publications, has heavily advocated equity goals. For example, *Tomorrow's Schools* states, "A Professional Development School selected because of its staff's commitment to bridging cultural divides can provide novices with systematic occasions to study equity within diversity" (p. 37). However, as with the Holmes research agenda more generally, "little research has been done on PDSes about diversity issues and school failure" (Valli, Cooper, & Frankes, 1996, p. 282).

The role of schools as agents of social and political reform is a tall order. It is not enough to advocate it. Local conditions and strategies must support its implementation: "district policies, as well as school structures, processes, schedules, and resources, must support the reforms; teachers must share, and have the power to enact the vision" (ibid., pp. 298–299). Even in schools where this is sincerely attempted, there are tremendous deep-seated barriers (such as power relationships and who benefits) in making headway (Oakes et al., 1997).

Furthermore, as we mentioned earlier in reference to initiatives on professional development infrastructure, it is increasingly clear that parent and community reform must be closely linked to teacher and school reform (Fullan & Watson, 1997). Promoting teacher professionalism not only must avoid widening the gap from parents, but also must explicitly embody how the gap could be narrowed.

With the publication of *Tomorrow's Schools*, the Holmes Group emphasized the importance of quality teaching for all children, stressing the need for educators to learn a great deal about students' backgrounds and cultures in order to teach them successfully. This means confronting issues of race and ethnicity as well as responding to issues of gender and disability—a still largely unfinished agenda.

One of the themes emerging across all the data sets was the belief that the Holmes Group was stronger in ideas than action, that it could have accomplished more if it had spent less time wrestling with words and more time developing and implementing an action plan. In the view of many respondents, the Holmes Group did not fulfill its considerable potential because it failed to pursue its own action agenda in any depth. The Holmes Group substituted writing papers for systematic lobbying or working to implement the agenda; "too much time and energy was devoted to finding the right word, as though the right word would move reform along." One faculty member spoke for many in stating, "The Holmes Group has the reputation in our institution as being strong on talk, weak on action." On the other hand, particularly in the first two books of the trilogy, the Holmes Group formulated powerful ideas, fostered dialogue and debate, and influenced the thinking of untold numbers.

> IN THE VIEW OF MANY RESPONDENTS, THE HOLMES GROUP DID NOT FULFILL ITS CONSIDERABLE POTENTIAL BECAUSE IT FAILED TO PURSUE ITS OWN ACTION AGENDA IN ANY DEPTH.

At the national level, the Holmes Group seems to have suffered some confusion about its role in relation to teacher education reform. Like various independent commissions, the Holmes Group produced major reports setting out, in general terms, an agenda for reform. The Holmes Group, on the other hand, was a group of educational "insiders," making recommendations that applied to their own institutions. To maintain credibility, they would have to be seen to be implementing their own agenda and assisting others to do the same. And yet, our data suggest that the Holmes Group as a national organization did not make the difficult but important shift from an agenda-creating body to an agenda-implementing body.

The degree to which the Holmes Group as an organization should have been active in fostering local implementation, especially during this initial 10-year period, however, is a debatable point. It could be argued that the main task was in formulating a compelling national agenda. Interviews with Holmes Group leaders indicate that Holmes never saw itself as a technical assistance organization. It built an agenda and expected the deans to deliver on it, interpreting it to suit their own unique contexts. In some cases, the expectations were fulfilled. A dean who had been successful in implementing the agenda described the relationship as follows: "The Holmes Group leadership provided the ideas, but it was up to us as deans to take action. I took a great deal of action. It caused discomfort, but it got us moving. I think the criticism that there is not an action agenda is in the eye of the beholder."

Not all deans, however, were able to make the changes on their own. Several deans and faculty members expressed frustration and disappointment; in the words of one dean, "I have reached out for help and support to the Holmes Group and it's been unresponsive." Many faculty in our study noted that they often left national meetings frustrated with the lack of progress on the action aspects of the agenda. For those institutions that were members of both the Holmes Group and the National Network for Educational Renewal (NNER), the lack of emphasis on action presented less of a problem. Holmes provided legitimacy and a framework, while NNER had more of an action agenda and expectation for accountability. The ideas and principles of reform in both networks were compatible.

Another perspective on the lack of action comes from deans of institutions who left the Holmes Group, several of whom noted that member institutions were not held accountable for implementing the agenda. In other words, although the original vision of the Holmes Group required a commitment to action at the local level, institutions were able to avoid such action, yet remain in the organization if they wished.

In considering the difficulties encountered with local implementation of the national agenda, faculty and deans in our interviews had several suggestions of how a national organization could support action.

- The most frequent suggestion was to increase the emphasis on networking and learning from the experiences of other schools and colleges of education and PDSes. Communication should be broad-based and bottom-up as well as top-down, so the leadership group understands members' views and the progress they are making in local sites.

- Focus more on implementation problems and on identifying strategies for overcoming such problems. Access the experience and learning of member colleges that are working with these ideas, both through publications such as the guidebook on strategies for increasing diversity in schools and colleges of education, or through workshop-type sessions in which problems are shared and solutions suggested. The work of Goodlad's National Network for Educational Renewal is perceived as a good example of providing hands-on work focused on action as well as ideas.

- Make use of national meetings to focus on strategies for action to move the agenda along and resolve problems with implementation.

- Provide support with documenting and evaluating progress at both the local and national levels to track progress and problems, and to provide evidence of success. Develop and coordinate a program of research which assesses and continually builds on what is learned.

ORGANIZATIONAL ISSUES

Analysis of data gathered through interviews and the survey reveals that within the Holmes Group, organizational issues created delays and barriers that often frustrated members.

Decision-making and communication in any such national organization would not be easy. In this case, when members are research universities in all parts of the country, with varying priorities and concerns, it has been especially difficult. Because the top priority of deans of education is dealing with their own schools, colleges, and departments of education, they rarely took the initiative in establishing and maintaining communication with the central Holmes office. Although some administrative support has always been available in the Holmes Group, it was never adequate and was seriously eroded in 1993 when Kathy Devaney, the senior staff member in charge of communication, passed away. No one had full-time responsibility for ensuring that the Holmes Group operated effectively as a consortium—that is, linking, representing, and supporting its members as they work to reform teacher education. Given the size and complexity of the agenda in which the Holmes Group is engaged, this limited organization and administrative capacity was a serious weakness.

Getting a new organization established often requires a more centralized Board of Directors and leadership. However, the Holmes Group leadership recognized by 1995, and our findings corroborate, that a more broadly based partnership, with a more inclusive leadership style and greater administrative resources, was required. Many respondents observed that the Holmes Group leadership seemed somewhat isolated from the members and that more organizational resources should be available to support communication and networking.

III. THE HOLMES GROUP IN THE BROADER POLICY CONTEXT

Policy contexts at the state and national levels are highly influential in shaping the agenda for reform, especially at a time of growing discontent with public institutions. The policy context for teacher education during the initial decade of reform (1985–1995) was complex and dynamic. Across the United States, the 1980s were characterized by two parallel but somewhat anomalous trends: at the same time the Holmes Group and other education professionals were developing and communicating a framework calling for more rigorous teacher preparation for teachers, many states were introducing policies that de-emphasized professional preparation for teachers. Caps on the number of hours in education courses and models for alternative certification are examples of policies that move in the opposite direction to those that would be proposed by most teacher educators and certainly by those in the Holmes Group. The Holmes Group was not alone in its recommendations; the Carnegie Forum (1986), the National Council for Accreditation of Teacher Education, and the National Board for Professional Teaching Standards all agreed on the need to strengthen professional preparation and agreed on at least some of the means for doing so. Yet policies directly counter to their recommendations cropped up increasingly across the country (Gideonse, 1992).

Berry and Catoe (1994) show how prescriptive state policies in South Carolina conflict with emerging standards of practice for teaching and with more challenging professional preparation programs:

> The state-mandated beginning teacher evaluation system (with its requirements of demonstrating 51 discrete, teaching behaviors in a 5-minute or less class period) is an aggravation and, to some extent, an anathema to the kinds of teaching and learning exemplified in [the new master's elementary program]. (p. 196)

Even state policy changes consistent with the Holmes Group agenda, such as requiring an undergraduate degree in arts and sciences or increasing internship requirements, were often enacted in a context that seemed highly critical of teacher education institutions, in that the emphasis was shifted from schools and colleges of education to faculties of arts and sciences, or to schools.

Clark (1992), in discussing teacher education policy in the 1980s, noted that the policy context reflected the low level of public confidence in the system of teacher education, a lack of confidence further exacerbated by the low status of teacher education within the university and disagreement among teacher educators themselves. The Holmes Group was also concerned that many schools of education in the country offered programs of low quality. The 1980s were characterized by a growing public agenda for educational improvement that appeared to be simple, feasible and cost-effective, involving testing teachers at entry and exit points, limiting the number of hours of pedagogical training, and establishing alternative routes for new sources of candidates. Such proposals were in contrast to the more rigorous proposals coming from the Holmes Group and other education leaders, proposals that involved longer and stronger (and more expensive) programs, as well as elaborate restructuring of field-based work through PDSes.

EVIDENCE FROM OUR DATA INDICATES THAT THE HOLMES GROUP WAS NOT HIGHLY ACTIVE IN THE POLICY ARENA. . . .

Throughout the decade of its existence, the Holmes Group has grappled with the problems of reforming education, and especially teacher education. As we have noted throughout the report, the main focus was on articulating the agenda for reform for both schools and colleges of education and their parent universities, extending as well into partnerships with local schools and school districts. Although Holmes targeted its own institutions, the expectation was that program reform in these major research universities would provide a new standard for the profession, and other institutions would be stimulated to move toward higher quality teacher preparation programs.

Other than the important contribution of its three public reports (the first two of which were influential), evidence from our data indicates that the Holmes Group was not highly active in the policy arena, particularly at the national and state levels. Interview data from those involved from the group's inception suggest that there was little extended discussion about Holmes playing a high-profile role in trying to influence policy. There were some links such as the Holmes president serving on the Carnegie Forum and on the board of the National Board for Professional Teaching Standards, or a founding Holmes dean moving to a senior position at the Educational Testing Service, but these did not represent systematic strategies to link Holmes with national policy developments.

The Holmes Group as a national body appears not to have taken action with regard to the legislative as opposed to the professional policy context, in that the Holmes Group did not speak or lobby against more anti-professional policy changes enacted in some states. Such changes included quick alternative certification programs and caps on professional studies. One long-time Holmes board member suggested that the group preferred to speak in favor of what they wanted to see rather than speak against what they disapproved of. On the other hand, a number of Holmes deans talked about their work in their own states, serving on state-level committees or providing advice to state officials and legislators, but the survey data suggest that this, too, was sporadic and personal rather than systematic.

It is unlikely that the Holmes Group had the legitimacy and the right organizational structure to play a more direct role in national and state policy development. For whatever reason, the Holmes Group did not wade into the policy debates involving the regulatory political role of the state or the internal policies of academe.

C. CONCLUSION

A more elaborate action-oriented conclusion is the focus of the next chapter. A very brief statement can be made here in relation to the three questions that guided our study, and the accomplishments of the Holmes Group.

1. How appropriate were the goals of the Holmes Group?

    The Holmes Group agenda in regard to teacher preparation might be described as concentrated in three areas: improving the arts and sciences preparation of teacher candidates, strengthening professional studies at schools and colleges of education, and providing more solid clinical preparation in PDSes. Colleges of education have a critical role in all three areas. Beyond this emphasis on teacher preparation, however, the Holmes Group also aimed at changing the conditions in schools for both teachers and students. The Holmes Group in so doing also sought to strengthen the research and development base for the teaching profession.

In general, we would concur with most other observers and commentators that the Holmes Group was indeed on the right track with the direction of its suggested reforms. Developing programs to increase the content knowledge of prospective teachers and improve their understanding of pedagogy, strengthening clinical education, and developing the research knowledge base —all these made good sense not only for the research universities in the Holmes Group but also for other teacher preparation institutions.

The shift in emphasis over the years in the priority and attention given to certain goals suggests that events led the Holmes Group to reconsider some goals and directions. The agenda, while remaining supportive of certain key principles, has for various reasons shifted over time. For example, the Holmes Group was initially strongly identified with recommendations for moving initial teacher preparation to the postbaccalaureate level and for establishing career ladders for teachers. *Tomorrow's Teachers* clearly stated that organizing members of the Holmes Group affirmed that "baccalaureate graduates would not be recommended for certification as teachers without a professional master's degree in education" (p. 74) and that the distinctions in training and responsibility between Professional Teachers and Instructors needed to remain clear (p. 75).

Within a few years, however, the emphasis had changed. Institutions identified problems with shifting to 5-year programs and other reform goals took priority. By 1995, what had originally been seen as a central feature of the Holmes agenda had assumed less importance. These adjustments seem to us to be sensible as the Holmes Group recognized that differences in local and state contexts meant that different routes had to be entertained in the pursuit of common principles.

2. What progress have member institutions made with the Holmes Group agenda?

Consistent with the theme of our report—that the agenda for reform of teacher education has barely been scratched—we could not say that substantial implementation has been accomplished, nor would we expect that on any scale. Individual institutions have been guided by the ideas in *Tomorrow's Teachers* and *Tomorrow's Schools*, and it appears that program changes are occurring. PDSes have been established by all Holmes Group members and in many other universities, albeit with the problems of implementation noted earlier. The research agenda for teacher education continues to lag behind, although many institutions have research projects underway. The influence of the PDS on other schools in the district, changes in the colleges of education's overall teacher preparation programs, and transforming incentives and the culture of the college as an institution all remain problematic.

3. What impact has the Holmes Group had on the field of teacher education beyond its own member institutions?

It is not, of course, strictly possible to isolate the impact of the Holmes Group from other reform initiatives and groups pushing for similar directions. Specifically, the Holmes Group and the NNER now share very similar agendas. However, we concur with most of our interviewees in concluding that Holmes has had considerable impact, both on the discourse about teacher education and also on action. To a large extent, the Holmes Group, with the publication of *Tomorrow's Teachers* in 1986, set the terms for ensuing debate about teacher education. One or both major Holmes Group publications are referenced in most articles about teacher education reform in the late 1980s and early 1990s. Furthermore, the ideas advocated by the Holmes Group have been widely adopted: even a cursory glance at teacher education journals shows a plethora of articles about PDSes and redesigned teacher education programs written by authors not associated with Holmes institutions.

MORE BROADLY, THE HOLMES GROUP HAS MANY SIGNIFICANT ACCOMPLISHMENTS TO ITS CREDIT.

More broadly, the Holmes Group has many significant accomplishments to its credit. As we have noted throughout this chapter, these include:

- the trilogy of reports: *Tomorrow's Teachers, Tomorrow's Schools,* and *Tomorrow's Schools of Education;*
- framing the teacher education reform debate; introducing and establishing PDS;
- stimulating and legitimizing partnerships between schools/school districts and universities;
- contributing to the enhancement of the status of schools, colleges, and departments of education within universities;
- providing direction and networking for local and regional teacher education reform efforts;
- strengthening, particularly through the Holmes Scholars program, minority representation among faculty in schools and colleges of education.

After a decade of pioneering work, the field of education is significantly better off because of the work of the Holmes Group and its success in bringing national attention to reform in teacher education.

However, the real question remains—has *anybody* had a major impact on the field of teacher education? Substandard practices persist in the shadows of spotlighted reform efforts such as the Holmes Group, the National Network for Educational Renewal, the Renaissance Group and others, speaking to the enormity and complexity of changing institutions that are a century old. What then are the issues facing the future of teacher education, and more especially—what are the prospects, *this time,* for real reform?

CHAPTER 3
THE FUTURE OF TEACHER EDUCATION: 1996-2006

If it takes a whole village to raise a child, can a whole nation change teacher education? We don't quite have the nation on board, but there is a remarkable convergence of forces coming together in 1996–1997. Recall, however, that there was great enthusiasm, fanfare, and confidence in 1985–1986 when the Carnegie and Holmes reports were released. What's different in 1996–1997? In answering this question, we consider what is needed, what's happening, and what's ahead.

WHAT'S NEEDED

Early in this report, we raised the question of whether or not society wants good teachers enough to advance the cause of teaching and teacher education. A major recommendation we have, whether for the Holmes Partnership or others, as John Goodlad and his colleagues have advocated, pertains to what needs to be done to educate society regarding the critical role of well-prepared teachers, who understand the public purpose of schooling in a democratic society. Acting on this moral imperative remains the highest priority.

Central to this priority is the recognition that teacher preparation is a subsidiary problem of the larger agenda of what role should schools, colleges, and departments of education play in wider systemic change. It is important that any strategy must be concerned with all the major pieces, even if it does not work on them all the time. In this sense, we agree with Joan Walsh (1997):

... [P]rojects must understand and have a strategy for addressing the interconnection of the many issues that contribute to persistent urban poverty: unemployment, crime, housing, school failure, family trouble. But that doesn't mean that they have to work on all of these issues at once. The best projects tackle what they are best positioned to make a difference on, and work out from there. Projects stall when they're paralyzed by the mandate to do too much. (p. 36)

Let us start with the larger problem of educational change. School reform has not been particularly successful either (and that indeed is part of the problem). We have had a broken front of 30 years of reform efforts and related research. The false but promising start of educational reform in the 1960s almost disappeared in the 1970s and early 1980s. A new cycle of reform, commencing around the time of the formation of the Holmes Group, is now beginning to produce new knowledge and insights about what makes for success. We will draw on some of this recent research to identify and illustrate the key components that must come together. These conclusions about successful school reform also have implications for successful teacher education reform.

A good place to start is the report on school restructuring, synthesizing 5 years of research in over 800 schools in 16 states (Newmann & Wehlage, 1995). The convergence of a small number of major components is critical in explaining reform. A combination of four factors was associated with successful school restructuring and increased student learning. The critical factors were:

- a vision of high-quality student learning;
- significant changes in teaching practice to support this vision of student learning;
- school organization capacity;
- external support.

Within these factors "professional learning communities were critical because they created opportunities for teachers to collaborate and help one another achieve the purpose" (p. 3). "External Support" was also essential when it provided "standards for learning of high intellectual quality . . . [and] sustained, school-wide staff development" (p. 4).

These findings are corroborated in other studies. Professional learning communities and collaborative work cultures must be, but usually are not, combined with external systems of standards and support (see also Cohen, 1995; Elmore, 1995; Fullan & Hargreaves, 1996; Hargreaves & Fullan, 1998; and McLaughlin & Talbert, 1993).

Put another way, school reform is also stalled. Through tremendous efforts on the part of small numbers of committed educators, major nationwide reform programs have produced pockets of success. However, such school initiatives are currently experiencing one or more of the following stalled effects:

THE RISE AND STALL OF EDUCATIONAL REFORM IS ESSENTIALLY A MATTER OF "HOPE ON HOLD," AND THE PROBLEM IS BECOMING PERVASIVE.

1. burnt-out teachers frustrated by the difficulty of, or lack of, progress;
2. problems in staying focused on, or clarifying, the vision in practice;
3. small groups of innovators being isolated from other educators in the school or school district—thus the failure to achieve whole school or whole district reform;
4. inability to disseminate the innovation on a wider scale without losing quality control.

The rise and stall of educational reform is essentially a matter of "hope on hold," and the problem is becoming pervasive.

Furthermore, as we have noted earlier, school reform and community reform must go hand in hand. Under conditions of poverty, including huge inequities across class and races, the development and mobilization of large numbers of caring adults is absolutely critical to the chances of success, and in this sense parent and community development must be closely linked to teacher development. Thus, any set of strategies for reform in teacher education must be concerned with connections to school and community reform more generally, even though it might focus on the preparation and continuous development of educators. Starting with teacher education, we know what the main components of reform entail:

- a stronger knowledge base for teaching and teacher education;
- attracting able, diverse, and committed students to the career of teaching;
- redesigning teacher preparation programs so that the linkages to arts and sciences, and to the field of practice, are both strengthened;
- reform in the working conditions of schools;
- the development and monitoring of external standards for programs as well as for teacher candidates and teachers on the job; and
- a rigorous and dynamic research enterprise focusing on teaching, teacher education, and on the assessment and monitoring of strategies.

Among other things, this amounts to transforming schools, colleges, and departments of education themselves; establishing education as a central and vital faculty within the university; creating and sustaining close working partnerships between universities and schools; and transforming schools and their communities (see also Darling-Hammond, 1997b).

The National Commission on Teaching and America's Future (NCTAF) has essentially captured this agenda in setting a "man-on-the-moon" benchmark:

We propose an audacious goal . . . by the year 2006, America will provide all students in the country with what should be their educational birthright: access to competent, caring, and qualified teachers. (p. vi)

The National Commission on Teaching and America's Future (NCTAF) has five major interlocking strategies formulated to accomplish this:

- Get serious about standards, for both students and teachers;
- Reinvent teacher preparation and professional development;
- Overhaul teacher recruitment, and put qualified teachers in every classroom;
- Encourage and reward knowledge and skill; and
- Create schools that are organized for student and teacher success.

Aside from our earlier warning that greater professionalism must encompass greater closeness to parents and the community —one that is based on *mutual* influence—the NCTAF platform is impressive. What is needed, then, is the specific work to accomplish this tremendously ambitious agenda. What can best express this at the micro and macro levels? Relative to the former, what is needed on the ground is the detailed design and operationalization of new teacher education programs as embedded in their school and district partnerships. These prototypes must struggle with how to learn from each other, but especially how best to broaden their influence by establishing two-way learning relationships with non-prototype (so to speak) schools.

AT THE MACRO LEVEL, WE NEED TO FIGURE OUT HOW TO REDUCE CLUTTER AND INCREASE COORDINATION.

At the macro level, we need to figure out how to reduce clutter and increase coordination. On the one hand, homogenous harmonization is neither possible nor desirable. On the other hand, the field is badly in need of more partnerships, greater coordination of initiatives, and more concentrated political resolve to carry the agenda forward in the face of great inertia. The politics of completing a commission report is one thing; the politics of establishing sustained pressure and support for implementation is another.

WHAT'S HAPPENING

If you like alphabet soup, you will love this section. At the national level, there are four major new developments which are mostly interrelated. They concern the newly formed Holmes Partnership (HP), the follow-up implementation of the National Commission on Teaching and America's Future (NCTAF) and three brand new major U.S. Department of Education initiatives: the reauthorization of Title V of the Higher Education Act, driven by a vision, "Shaping the Profession that Shapes America's Future" (SPSAF); the National Partnership for Excellence and Accountability in Teaching (NPEAT); and the creation of a National Research Center on Policy and Teaching Excellence (NRCPTE).

1. THE HOLMES PARTNERSHIP (HP)

The Holmes Group recognized many of the problems we identified in our assessment of its work. To move beyond the stall it needed to generate new power and momentum, develop a more comprehensive program of policy action, build greater organization capacity, and establish alliances and partnerships with other major players. It has done just that taking the following actions at its annual meeting in January 1997.

First, the Holmes Group was renamed the *Holmes Partnership* to signify that any further action must focus on reconstituting the school of education "in partnership with schools" and "in partnership with other national groups."

Second, the *goals* of the Holmes Partnership were recalibrated. While the Holmes Group stalled, the ideas did not die. The total number of goals in the trilogy of publications was about 20 —too many to make operational. The new Holmes Partnership formally adopted six goals:

Goal 1:   **High-Quality Professional Preparation** (provide exemplary programs that demonstrate attention to

	the needs of diverse children and youth, and that reflect research and best practice)
Goal 2:	**Simultaneous Renewal** (of schools and of the education of teachers through strong partnerships)
Goal 3:	**Equity, Diversity, and Cultural Competence** (actively work on equity by recruiting, preparing, and sustaining diverse faculty in schools and schools of education)
Goal 4:	**Scholarly Inquiry and Programs of Research** (conduct and disseminate a program of research to continually inform policy and practice)
Goal 5:	**Faculty Development** (provide high-quality doctoral programs and other forms of advanced professional development)
Goal 6:	**Policy Initiation** (engage in policy analysis and advocacy).

Third, new *governance* was established in the form of a broadly representative board of directors, five at-large members, 10 regional representatives, and seven partner representatives from national groups. The board has a five-member executive. In addition, officers of the partnership include a president (Nancy Zimpher), five vice-presidents (one from each region), and an executive director (Frank Murray).

Fourth, an elaborate *organization and network* of actions have been established to work on strategies to implement the six goals including: five levels [local, state, regional, national, (and soon) international]; annual national as well as regional working sessions; communications involving listservs, websites, and a repository for documents.

Fifth, the HP is expanding to include *national partners.* Seven have joined up to this point:

- American Association of Colleges for Teacher Education (AACTE)
- American Federation of Teachers (AFT)

- National Board for Professional Teaching Standards (NBPTS)
- National Council for Accreditation of Teacher Education (NCATE)
- National Education Association (NEA)
- National Policy Board for Educational Administration (NPBEA)
- National Staff Development Council (NSDC)

Several other national partners are being recruited.

Sixth, the HP aspires to become a national center for *research* on teacher education, planning to document, monitor, and evaluate developments in teacher education inside and outside Holmes' work. HP will focus on creating a strategic action agenda to ensure that it meets the goals that it has established. The work will be conducted in teams at the local, state, and regional levels through a "temporary system" of school and university participants who select and bid to carry out different tasks. A board retreat was held in August 1997 to chart a series of "design options" and to place those selected on a timeline and 5-year budgetary plan. There is a great deal of interest among HP members in participating in this multi-year, multifaceted strategic research agenda.

Seventh, new intensive partnerships devoted to *urban teacher education* will be launched as part of the Urban Network for Improving Teacher Education, II (UNITE II). UNITE I, unconnected to Holmes, consisted of nine schools of education which operated over a 3-year period (1993–1996) focusing on leadership, program development in partnership with schools, and faculty development (see Thiessen & Howey, 1998). UNITE II has been incorporated into HP, and will intensify these efforts with as many as 40–50 urban partnerships (a subset of HP, if you like) which will engage in program development, research, and dissemination in relation to three goals: (1) recruiting and preparing qualified teachers for urban schools, (2) focusing on high-performance teaching and learning, and (3) addressing directly the conditions and professional culture in both P–12 schools and schools and colleges of education to support teaching and learning. The concept is to establish a national program of improvement-oriented research involving collaborative teams of professors and school-based professionals.

Eighth, HP will maintain and greatly enhance the successful Holmes Scholars program designed to recruit and support future school of education professoriate from underrepresented groups.

In sum, the Holmes Partnership has acted, at least in its initial design, to address the gaps identified in our case study and is well positioned to act more systematically on its original and enhanced mandate.

2. NCTAF IMPLEMENTATION

Most commissions report, cause temporary excitement, and fade. Not so with NCTAF. An implementation secretariat is carrying on the work under the direction of Linda Darling-Hammond, the executive director of the commission. Twelve states have signed on "to work as partners with the commission . . . to create new policies and practices for dramatically improving the quality of teaching" (Darling-Hammond, 1997a).

> To become a partner state, each state was asked to submit a proposal that showed a statewide commitment to implementing a teacher quality agenda in the areas outlined in *What Matters Most,* and endorsements from the governor's office, chief state school officer, state board of education, and key education leaders. Each partner state agreed to assemble a broad-based policy group that would ensure the involvement of key stakeholders, including representatives from the governor's office; relevant state education agencies; boards having authority for teacher education as well as elementary, secondary, and higher education; professional associations; state legislators; leaders from the business community; and other public education and community advocates. Each state's policy group is responsible for receiving the results of a policy inventory that examines the full range of teacher-related issues—recruitment, preparation, licensing, in-

duction, certification, and ongoing professional development—as well as broader issues of student standards and school reform. (Darling-Hammond, 1997, p. 6)

The first year of work, already underway, includes:

1. creating networking opportunities so that state policy teams can share strategies, progress, and experiences;
2. developing and leading a policy inventory process whereby each state collects, analyzes, and reports information that outlines the status of teaching and teacher quality in the state; and
3. assisting states in using the policy inventory process to deepen public and practitioner understanding of the issues and to create state-level action plans to pursue a teacher development agenda linked to other school reforms (Darling-Hammond, 1997, p. 7).

Recall that the commission set a 10-year benchmark that by 2006, every student in the country will have a caring and competent teacher. There is a sense of urgency as the commission develops what it calls "far-reaching implementation plans."

Enter the Department of Education with three major initiatives: Reauthorization of Title V, NPEAT, and NRCPTE.

3. REAUTHORIZATION OF TITLE V—THE HIGHER EDUCATION ACT

As we write, major developments are underway to reauthorize Title V by providing policy impetus and corresponding resources for reforming teacher education in the country. In a discussion document, "Shaping the Profession that Shapes America's Future" (SPSAF), which takes its cue from NCTAF, the remarkable statement is made that the "front-end" of teacher education deserves the lion's share of attention (remarkable in that we have consistently observed that there does not appear to be the political will to take initial teacher education seriously):

The task is clear. Fundamentally, we must connect in a powerful way the quest for improved student achievement with the demand for increased teacher performance. The nation must move beyond its piecemeal and fragmented approaches to teacher development to create frameworks for policy and practice that comprehensively and coherently connect the different stages of a teacher's career (recruitment, preparation, induction, and ongoing professional development) to national, state, and district education goals. Colleges and universities, schools, school districts, governors and legislatures, state departments of education, state higher education commissions, and the U.S. Department of Education all need to address teacher development as a priority issue.

The U.S. Department of Education, for its part, must address all of these issues of teacher quality. One medium through which we can advance our teacher development vision is the Higher Education Act, whose reauthorization is scheduled for this year. Title V of this law currently authorizes numerous, disconnected programs relating to the professional development of teachers, only one of which receives funding. We have the opportunity now to create a strong Title V. However, instead of addressing all aspects of teacher development in this title, our proposal for its reauthorization will focus a the front-end of the professional development continuum—the recruitment, preparation, and induction of teachers and principals. (U.S. Department of Education, 1997, p. 9)

On July 17, 1997, President Clinton announced the Department of Education's Title V reauthorization proposal at the NAACP conference, calling it an initiative "to attract talented people of all backgrounds into teaching at low-income schools across the nation, and to dramatically improve the quality of teaching and preparation given our future teacher" (July 17, press release). The department has since transmitted its proposed legislation to Congress, where it awaits consideration by the House and Senate.

The initiative has two parts, for which the administration requests a total of $350 million over 5 years. Part A of the proposed legislation would authorize grants to "lighthouse partnerships"

---

between exemplary teacher preparation institutions, school districts, and other higher education institutions. The program would seek to identify and spread best practices in teacher education and would promote K–12 educators' vital role in designing and implementing effective teacher preparation programs:

> This initiative will provide competitive 5-year grants to 10–15 national "lighthouse" models of excellence—institutions of higher education that operate the highest quality teacher education programs. Each institution receiving a "lighthouse" grant will use a majority of these resources to help 8–15 other institutions of higher education improve their teacher preparation programs, helping to improve the preparation of future teachers at 150 institutions of higher education across the nation. These institutions must place a large number of graduates in high-poverty urban or rural schools. (July 17, press release)

Part B would authorize grants to partnerships between institutions of higher education and school districts in high-poverty urban and rural areas to recruit teachers and prepare them well. The partnerships would design recruitment and preparation programs to fit their teaching needs, providing both scholarships and, if necessary, support services to potential teachers. The administration estimates that the recruitment partnerships would support the recruitment of 35,000 teachers over the next 5 years to teach in underserved urban and rural schools.

It is still too early to tell if the actual reauthorization of Title V will receive political support and the allocation of significant resources to the redesign of teacher education programs. For the first time, however, political support exists on a wide scale from the president, many state governors, nearly all of the national education associations, and the U.S. Department of Education itself.

4. THE NATIONAL PARTNERSHIP FOR EXCELLENCE AND ACCOUNTABILITY IN TEACHING (NPEAT)

The United States Department of Education issued a request for proposals in spring 1997 for a $24 million, 5-year initiative on teacher education and continuous professional development. As stated in the request:

> The Partnership shall facilitate national efforts to support and sustain long-term improvements in teaching preparation and career-long learning; identify/develop a variety of proven, replicable teacher preparation and professional development programs; identify/develop effective programs to advance teacher accountability; conduct research on the incentives and impediments for positive change in teaching and its contexts; and, carry out technical assistance and dissemination activities. (U.S. Department of Education, 1997a)

One contract will be awarded, up to $4 million in Year 1 and $5 million for each of the four subsequent years. An award is expected to be granted in 1997. NPEAT will provide an opportunity for some of the critical issues identified by HP and NCTAF to be addressed.

5. THE NATIONAL RESEARCH CENTER ON POLICY AND TEACHING EXCELLENCE (NRCPTE)

The Department of Education also issued a call for proposals in spring 1997 for a new 5-year, $7.5 million national research center that will investigate policy-making and policy structures designed to achieve excellence in teaching. The center will look at policies and policy-making at all levels of government with an eye to improving the quality of teaching. Among its mandates is to "conduct a program of research and development that will aid policymakers throughout the nation at all levels of government and all levels of the educational system . . . to achieve the goal of teaching excellence and ensure continuous effort related to that goal." An award is expected soon with work to begin in 1997–1998.

WHAT'S AHEAD

Never before has teacher education experienced such a massive outpouring of political and fiscal action. Are we witnessing systemic synergy or considerable clutter? On the positive side, the agendas of the various groups and initiatives referred to in this report are essentially compatible. There is a philosophical, programmatic and strategic convergence of opinion about what needs to be done, and how urgent the problem is. Also positive is the predisposition of the different players to join in partnership in relation to policy and funding opportunities. Finally, there has been a great deal of initial work on the ground (for example, in Holmes and in Goodlad's National Network of Educational Renewal) which has resulted in a wide range of local capacity and commitment ready to link into and otherwise be mobilized by appropriate state, regional, and national strategies.

On the negative side is the nagging feeling that we are dealing with a reform proposition so profound that the teaching profession itself, along with the culture of schools and schools of education, will have to undergo total transformation in order for substantial progress to be made—that the agenda is much, much deeper than many realize. Included in this transformation is the growing realization that the walls of the school are tumbling down, requiring teachers and principals to radically reframe their relationship to parents and the community, governments, technology, the corporate sector, and the teaching profession as a whole (Hargreaves and Fullan, 1998).

We asked at the beginning of this chapter, "what's different about 1996–1997, compared to 1986" when Holmes started. The Holmes Group, a decade ago, was a pioneer in launching an ambitious agenda into uncharted territory which enjoyed little political favor either at the policy level, or at the level of the institutional politics of schools, colleges, and departments of education and their universities. A good deal was accomplished as individual institutions mobilized for reform, and as the Holmes collective articulated the trilogy of books. As far as implementation is concerned, however, we concluded that teacher education reform was introduced, but not substantially acted on. Right now, in 1997, reforming the profession of teaching is still a fragile and fledging proposition.

There is a difference as we approach the second decade of reform. There has never been a greater convergence of political and programmatic agreement, energy, and sense of urgency that immediate and sustained action on a comprehensive scale must take place. It is underway, and we have never seen the likes of it in the history of the teaching profession.

At the same time, there are many opportunities to slip "betwixt the cup and the lip." States are differentially interested and/or wrongheaded about teacher education reform, and it is at the state level where the policy responsibility lies (on the other hand, some states like the 12 that have joined NCTAF are willing to commit to an agenda of detailed implementation).

Will states and universities bite the bullet in closing those schools and colleges of education, among the almost 1,300 that exist, which should not stay in business? Are schools of education and their universities actually capable of going through with the internal reculturing of incentives, rewards, and reorganization necessary to become effective partners? Can schools and districts change to build the kinds of organization and infrastructures necessary to support the new profession envisaged in the current reform agenda? How will we contend with the practical pressures of hiring substandard teachers in times of certain shortages over the next decade?

We say all of this only to stress how truly profound the agenda is. It is every bit the crisis that the medical profession faced in

1910 when Abraham Flexner found it in a state of disrepair. Seymour Sarason observed that the medical profession and society take a different attitude to the problem of curing cancer than they do to the problem of addressing the ills of education. Curing cancer is seen as a complex proposition that will take decades of attention; people get busy working intensively on the problem. Beyond rhetoric and episodic commissions, sustained attention to teacher education reform has so far turned out to be politically unattractive. If society can devote itself to decades of energy to solve the many forms of cancer, we could do the same for reforming teacher education and the profession of teaching.

Only a feet-to-the-fire sustained effort taking at least a decade of intensive work by many partners has any chance of making headway. We have never been in a better position than now to take the actions required. We have a chance for the first time of really bringing the teaching profession into the postmodern age.

We *could* do this but then again, we may not. And that is what the rise and stall of reform in teacher education is all about. The period 1996–2006 will turn out to be the defining decade, not only for teacher education, and not only for the entire teaching profession, but also for the schools in the nation.

REFERENCES

Andrew, M. D. (1990). Differences between graduates of four-year and five-year teacher preparation programs. *Journal of Teacher Education, 41*(2), 45–51.

Andrew, M. D., & Schwab, R. L. (1995). Has reform in teacher education influenced teacher performance? An outcome assessment of graduates of eleven teacher education programs. *Action in Teacher Education, 17*(3), 43–53.

Berry, B., & Catoe, S. (1994). Creating PDS: Policy and practice in South Carolina's PDS initiatives. In L. Darling-Hammond (Ed.), *PDS: Schools for developing a profession.* New York: Teachers College Press.

Boyer, E. L. (1983). *High school.* New York: Harper & Row.

Carnegie Forum. (1986). *A nation prepared: Teachers for the 21st century.* New York: Author.

Case, C. W., Lanier, J. E., & Miskel, C. G. (1986, July–August). The Holmes Group report: Impetus for gaining professional status for teachers. *Journal of Teacher Education, 37*(4), 36–43.

Clark, D. L. (1992). Leadership in policy development by teacher educators: Search for a more effective future. In H. D. Gideonse (Ed.), *Teacher education policy: Narratives, stories, and cases.* Albany: State University of New York Press.

Clements, M. (1987, November–December). Dilemmas of the Holmes report. *Social Education, 51*(7), 509–512.

Cohen, D. K. (1995). What is the system in systemic reform? *Educational Researcher, 24*(9), 11–17, 31.

Cornbleth, C. (1987, November–December). Knowledge in curriculum and teacher education. *Social Education, 51*(7), 513–516.

Darling-Hammond, L. (1997a). National commission on teaching and America's future: Final progress report. New York: Teachers College, Columbia University.

Darling-Hammond, L. (1997b). *The right to learn.* San Francisco: Jossey-Bass.

Darling-Hammond, L., & Goodwin, A. L. (1993). Progress toward professionalism in teaching. In G. Cawelti (Ed.), *Challenges and achievements of American education: 1993 Yearbook of the Association for Supervision and Curriculum Development.* Alexandria, VA: ASCD.

Darling-Hammond, L., Wise, A. E., & Klein, S. P. (1995). *A license to teach: Building a profession for 21st-century schools.* Boulder, CO: Westview Press.

Elmore, R. F. (1995). Structural reform in educational practice. *Educational Researcher, 24*(9), 23–26.

Firestone, W. A. (1994). Redesigning teacher salary systems for educational reform. *American Educational Research Journal, 31*(3), 549–574.

Fullan, M. (1993). *Change forces: Probing the depths of educational reform.* London: Falmer Press.

Fullan, M. (1997). *What's worth fighting for in the principalship* (2nd. ed.). New York: Teachers College Press; Toronto: Ontario Public School Teachers' Federation.

Fullan, M. (1998). Leadership for change in faculties of education. In D. Thiessen & K. Howey (Eds.), *Agents, Provocateurs: Reform-Minded Leaders for Schools of Education.* Washington, DC: American Association of Colleges for Teacher Education.

Fullan, M., & Hargreaves, A. (1996). *What's worth fighting for in your school* (rev. ed.). New York: Teachers College Press; Toronto: Ontario Public School Teachers' Federation.

Fullan, M., Watson, N., with Kilcher, A. (1997). *Building infrastructures for professional development: An assessment of early progress.* New York: Rockefeller Foundation.

Gehrke, N. J. (1991). Simultaneous improvement of schooling and the education of teachers: Creating a collaborative consciousness. *Metropolitan Universities, 2*(1), 43–50.

Gideonse, H. D. (1992). *Teacher education policy: Narratives, stories, and cases.* Albany: State University of New York Press.

Gideonse, H. D. (1996). Holmes Group III: Responsible in goals; remiss in practicalities. *Journal of Teacher Education, 47*(2), 147–152.

Goodlad, J. I. (1984). *A place called school.* New York: McGraw-Hill.

Goodlad, J. I. (1990). *Teachers for our nation's schools.* San Francisco: Jossey-Bass.

Goodlad, J. I. (1994). *Educational renewal: Better teachers, better schools.* San Francisco: Jossey-Bass.

Grant, C. A. (1990, Winter). Barriers and facilitators to equity in The Holmes Group. *Theory into Practice, 29*(1), 50–54.

Hargreaves, A. (1995). Towards a social geography of teacher education. In N. K. Shimahara & I. Z. Holowinsky (Eds.), *Teacher education in industrialized nations.* New York: Garland.

Hargreaves, A. (1996). *Ten years after: An evaluation of the Holmes Group.* Presentation to the annual meeting of the American Education Research Association, Washington, DC.

Hargreaves, A., & Fullan, M. (1998). *What's worth fighting for "out there."* New York: Teachers College Press; Toronto: Ontario Public School Teachers' Federation.

Howey, K., & Zimpher, N. (1989). *Profiles of preservice teacher education.* Albany: Albany State University of New York.

Howey, K. (1996). Revisiting the purpose of PDS. *Contemporary Education, LXVII*(4), 180–186.

Howey, K. (1990, Winter). This issue. *Theory into Practice, 29*(1), 2–5.

Irvine, J. J. (1994). *Creating and sustaining diverse communities: The challenge of the Holmes Group. An evaluation of the Holmes equity agenda.* East Lansing, MI: The Holmes Group.

Jackson, P. W. (1987, Spring). Facing our ignorance. *Teachers College Record, 88*(3), 384–389.

Johnson, W. R. (1987, Summer). Empowering practitioners: Holmes, Carnegie, and the lessons of history. *History of Education Quarterly, 27*(2), 221–240.

Judge, H. (1982). *American graduate schools of education: A view from abroad.* New York: Ford Foundation.

Judge, H. (1987, Spring). Another view from abroad. *Teachers College Record, 88*(3), 394–399.

Judge, H., Carriedo, R., & Johnson, S. M. (1995). Review of *PDS in Michigan State University.* Lansing: Michigan State University.

Labaree, D. F. (1992). Power, knowledge, and the rationalization of teaching: A genealogy of the movement to professionalize teaching. *Harvard Educational Review, 62*(2) 123–154.

Labaree, D. F. (1995). A disabling vision: Rhetoric and reality in *Tomorrow's Schools of Education. Teachers College Record, 97*(2), 166–205.

Labaree, D. F., & Pallas, A. M. (1996). Dire straits: The narrow vision of the Holmes Group. *Educational Researcher, 25*(4), 25–28.

Lanier, J. (1996). *Ten years after: An evaluation of the Holmes Group.* Presentation to the annual meeting of the American Educational Research Association, Washington, DC.

Lanier, J., & Featherstone, J. (1988, November). A new commitment to teacher education. *Educational Leadership,* 18–22.

Martin, J. R. (1987, Spring). Reforming teacher education, rethinking liberal education. *Teachers College Record, 88*(3), 406–410.

Mathews, D. (1996). *Is there a public for public schools?* Dayton, OH: Kettering Foundation Press.

McLaughlin, M., & Talbert, J. (1993). Contexts that matter for teaching and learning. Stanford, CA: Center for Research on the Context of Secondary School Teaching.

Murray, F. B. (1993). "All or none" criteria for PDS. *Educational Policy, 7*(1), 61–73.

National Board for Professional Teaching Standards (NBPTS). (n.d.). *What teachers should know and be able to do.* Detroit: Author.

National Commission on Teaching and America's Future. (1996). *What matters most: Teaching for America's future.* Washington, DC: Author.

Newmann, F., & Wehlage, G. (1995). *Successful school restructuring.* Madison, WI: Center on Organization and Restructuring of Schools.

Nutting, W. C. (1985, February). A follow-up appraisal of professional development centers after six years of collaboration. Paper presented at the annual meeting of the Association of Teacher Educators, Las Vegas, NV.

Nystrand, R. O. (1991). *PDS: Toward a new relationship for schools and universities* (Trends and Issues Paper No. 4). Washington, DC: ERIC Clearinghouse on Teacher Education.

Oakes, J., Wells, A. S., Yonezawa, S., & Ray, K. (1997). Equity lessons from detracking schools. In A. Hargreaves (Ed.), *Rethinking educational change with heart and mind.* Alexandria, VA: Association for Supervision and Curriculum Development, 43–72.

Rury, J., & Mirel, J. (1997). The political economy of urban education. *Review of Education, 22,* 49–112.

Rustique, E., & Darling-Hammond, L. (1996, January). Extended teacher preparation programs: A review of the literature. Draft paper prepared for the National Commission on Teaching and

America's Future. New York: National Commission on Teaching and America's Future.

Sarason, S. B., Davidson, K. S., & Blatt, B. (1986). *The preparation of teachers: An unstudied problem in education* (rev. ed.). Cambridge, MA: Brookline.

Schlechty, P. C., & Joslin, A. W. (1984). Images of schools. *Teachers College Record, 86*(1), 156–170.

Sizer, T. R. (1984). *Horace's compromise: The dilemma of the American high school.* Boston: Houghton-Mifflin.

The Holmes Group. (1986). *Tomorrow's teachers: A report of the Holmes Group.* East Lansing, MI: Author.

The Holmes Group. (1990). *Tomorrow's schools: Principles for the design of PDS.* East Lansing, MI: Author.

The Holmes Group. (1995). *Tomorrow's schools of education: A report of the Holmes Group.* East Lansing, MI: Author.

Thiessen, D., & Howey, K. (Eds.). (1998). *Agents, provocateurs: Reform-minded leaders for schools of education.* Washington, DC: American Association of Colleges for Teacher Education.

Tyson, H. (1995). Holmes Group: Revolutionary talk, timid proposals. *ATE Newsletter, 28*(6), 3, 6.

U.S. Department of Education. (1997a). A partnership of excellence and accountability in teaching. Request for Proposal. Washington, DC: Author.

U.S. Department of Education. (1997b). Shaping the profession that shapes America's future. Initial ideas on teacher development across America and the reauthorization of Title V of the Higher Education Act. Washington, DC: Author.

Valli, L., Cooper, D., & Frankes, L. (1996). PDS and equity: A critical analysis of rhetoric and research. *Review of Research in Education, 22,* 251–304.

Walsh, J. (1997). *Stories of renewal: Community building and the future of urban America.* New York: The Rockefeller Foundation.

Welch, M. (1993). Commentary: Faculty partnerships can make special ed part of the main. *The Holmes Group Forum, VIII*(1), 17–18.

Whitford, B. L., & Hovda, R. A. (1986). Schools as knowledge work organizations: Perspectives and implications from the new management literature. *The Urban Review, 18*(1), 52–70.

Winitzky, N., Stoddart, T., & O'Keefe, P. (1992). Great expectations: Emergent PDS. *Journal of Teacher Education, 43*(1), 3–18.

Yinger, R. J., & Hendricks, M. S. (1990). An overview of reform in Holmes Group institutions. *Journal of Teacher Education, 41*(2), 21–26.